D1488470

LABELING MADNESS

Thomas J. Scheff is Professor of Sociology
at The University of California at Santa Barbara.

Edited by
Thomas J. Scheff

LABELING MADNESS

RC 437.5
.S33

A SPECTRUM BOOK

PRENTICE-HALL, INC., ENGLEWOOD CLIFFS, N.J.

Library of Congress Cataloging in Publication Data

Scheff, Thomas J   comp.
  Labeling madness.

  (A Spectrum book)
  Includes bibliographical references.
  CONTENTS: Labeling theory as ideology and as science:
Scheff, T. J. Schizophrenia as ideology. Scheff, T. J.
On reason and sanity. Scheff, T. J. [etc.]
   1. Psychiatry—Philosophy—Addresses, essays, lectures.
2. Psychology, Pathological—Classification—
Addresses, essays, lectures. I. Title.
[DNLM: 1. Mental disorders. WM100 S316L]
RC437.5.S33   616.8'9'001   75-2207
ISBN 0-13-517367-1
ISBN 0-13-517359-0 pbk.

INDIANA
UNIVERSITY
LIBRARY

NORTHWEST

© 1975 by PRENTICE-HALL, INC.
ENGLEWOOD CLIFFS, NEW JERSEY

A SPECTRUM BOOK

All rights reserved.
No part of this book may be reproduced
in any form or by any means
without permission in writing from the publisher.

10 9 8 7 6 5 4 3 2 1

Printed in the United States of America

PRENTICE-HALL INTERNATIONAL, INC. (*London*)
PRENTICE-HALL OF AUSTRALIA PTY., LTD. (*Sydney*)
PRENTICE-HALL OF CANADA, LTD. (*Toronto*)
PRENTICE-HALL OF INDIA PRIVATE LIMITED (*New Delhi*)
PRENTICE-HALL OF JAPAN, INC. (*Tokyo*)

For Jane

CONTENTS

INTRODUCTION

This book presents a discussion of some recent developments in the labeling theory of mental illness. My first application of labeling theory to the problem of madness was in *Being Mentally Ill*, published in 1966. Two developments since that time have led to this book. First, since 1966 many articles directly relevant to labeling theory have been published. Some of these articles are critiques; most are reports of empirical studies that provide evidence for or against the validity of theory. These concerns are represented in Part I of this book. The second development involved my own thinking about the problem of madness. After the publication of *Being Mentally Ill*, I began to consider the problem of bringing about change in the system I had described. I became convinced that to change the social institution of madness, it would be necessary to approach the problem not only on the social-system level, as labeling theory does, but also on the psychological level. For this reason, I sought a psychological theory that would complement labeling theory rather than contradict it, and so allow a more comprehensive approach to the problem. These concerns are reflected in Part II of this book.

The chapters in Part I deal with the current status of labeling theory as ideology and as science. Chapter 1, "Schizophrenia as Ideology," presents a brief outline of labeling theory, and compares its ideological implications with those of the medical model. Chapter 2, "On Reason and Sanity: Some Political Implications of Psychiatric Thought," uses the labeling theory of mental illness, and studies based on it, as an ideology in order to point out some of the politically conservative elements implicit in current psychiatric thought. Just as the medical model of mental illness can be seen as the official ideology of the psychiatric establishment, labeling theory can be seen as the counter-ideology. Chapter 3, "The Labeling Theory of Mental Illness," deals, in somewhat greater detail, with the scientific status of the theory. It responds to the various critiques of labeling theory, and evaluates the studies that provide evidence for and against the theory. The remaining three chapters in Part I provide examples of the kinds of studies that give empirical support to the labeling theory of mental illness.

As I indicated above, labeling theory provides a description of the social system for dealing with madness. It concerns the social institution of madness as it exists in contemporary Western societies. Its emphasis is on describing the actual state of affairs, the way that society reacts to "mental illness," and how this reaction contributes to the problem. In addition to being a description, labeling theory also involves a critique, a protest against the practices it describes. Implicit in labeling theory is the argument that conditions need not and should not be the way they are. Part I thus contains a statement of the problem: the need for change in conceptualizing and dealing with madness in our society.

Part II explores possible solutions to the problem raised in the discussion in Part I. What are the sources of labeling in society and in the individual, and what are the alternatives? Whereas Part I is concerned with conditions as they are, Part II deals with possible sources of these conditions, and ways in which they might be changed. Inasmuch as Part II represents a new departure in my thinking about madness, I want to discuss further the ideas that led me in this direction.

The problem raised in Part II concerns change: how can we change the social institution of madness? As a result of my investigations of mental hospitals during the decade from 1960 to 1970, I became aware of one fallacy about change, which I came to think of as the psychological fallacy. This fallacy, according to my thinking, is that individual treatment is the key to the problem of madness. Although I agree that individual treatment is often indispensable, its effects usually do not last long unless changes occur in the individual's milieu that support the changes in his personality. Although there have been some notable exceptions, such as Therapeutic Community, most treatment programs in Western societies are ineffectual because they are based upon the psychological fallacy.

As I thought about the problem of creating change in the institution of madness, it slowly became clear to me that there was another fallacy—as important as, and opposite to, the psychological fallacy—which I think of as the sociological fallacy. This is the idea that for social change to occur, all that is necessary is to create new institutions without having to change individuals. This basic idea operates on a small scale in utopian societies and, currently, in countercultural communes. On a large scale, it seems to dominate most political revolutions. A group of people withdraw from or overthrow one set of institutions, which they found oppressive, in order to create a new set of institutions more in keeping with their ideals. The root of the oppression, they argue, is not in individuals but in defective institutions.

The fallacy in this argument is that the institutions of the former society are smuggled into the new society through the personalities of the participants. Authoritarianism, possessiveness, and violence may, as the reformers argue, be produced by the old institutions, but they do not disappear overnight. Utopias and communes often don't last, partly because of the pressure of the host society, but probably due mostly to the disruptiveness of the old personality patterns on the new institutions. Similar comments can be made about many of the changes brought about by political revolution. A new group comes to power, at times bringing with them radically new institutions. But in most cases, the old institutions survive in the new society: elites, bureaucracy, rigidity, oppression. *La plus sa change; la plus le meme chose.*

What seems necessary for long-lasting, fundamental change in social institutions is a combination of both individual and societal change. Changes in individuals must take place in a context that encourages congruent changes in the social structure. Similarly, programs that envision institutional change must also deal somehow with the personalities of the individuals who are to live with the new institutions. Apparently, it is no simple matter to combine these two levels of change. When Moses led the children of Israel out of Egypt, he had them sojourn for forty years in the desert. He waited for the generation who were born slaves to die, lest they bring the slave mentality into the land of milk and honey. A new generation, born free, would create a new society. Although this idea is more advanced than the thinking in many current utopias, in that it attempts to deal with change at both the individual and institutional level, it is still incomplete. From what we know now of the socialization process (see the section on child raising in Chapter 7 of this volume), we would guess that the adults who raised the children in the desert would have inadvertently passed on their own personality traits to the new generation.

The Chinese Communist revolution may prove to be an exception to the above strictures. It is still difficult to gain an impartial picture of this revolution because information concerning it is highly polarized. Reports from China grossly exaggerate its virtues, and reports from the West, its defects. Nevertheless, it appears that during their long struggle for power, from 1921 to 1949, basic changes may have taken place in the personalities of most of the Chinese Communist leadership, and much of the rank and file. The Chinese Communists appear to have devised group techniques, such as Speak Bitterness, Self-criticism–Criticism, and Thought Reform, that lead to change at both the individual and social level. It also appears, if contemporary reports about China are even partially accurate, that fundamental changes in virtually all of the institutions of Chinese society have taken place since the revolution. Since the example of China seems crucial for our thesis, it would be very helpful to do further research on the amount and kind of changes that have occurred in Chinese society at the individual and social level, and how these types of change are related one to the other.

The problem of change at the individual and societal level is dealt with in Part II of this book. Chapter 7, "Labeling, Emotion, and Individual Change," begins with a discussion of the sources of labeling in modern societies, and then formulates a relationship among emotional repression, discharge, and individual and collective change. The remaining chapters in Part II provide support for the thesis of Chapter 7.

PART I
Labeling Theory as Ideology
and as Science

1

SCHIZOPHRENIA AS IDEOLOGY
Thomas J. Scheff

Chapter 1 offers a brief statement of the labeling theory of mental illness. This theory provides a way of conceptualizing mental illness which is an alternative to the "medical model." The term "mental illness"—and its associated concepts, "symptoms," "diagnosis," "therapy," "patient," and so on—is a product of the medical model. Labeling theory proposes an entirely different set of concepts for dealing with the same behavior: "residual rules," "rule breaking," "deviant role," and so on, as indicated in the first three chapters below. In addition to summarizing the labeling position, this chapter also outlines an analysis of the medical model as an ideology that tends to uphold the social status quo, an analysis that is continued in Chapter 2.

In lieu of beginning this chapter with a (necessarily) abstract discussion of a concept, *the public order,* I shall invite the reader to consider a *gedanken* experiment that will illustrate its meaning. Suppose that in your next conversation with a stranger, instead of looking at his eyes or mouth, you scrutinize his ear. Although the deviation from ordinary behavior is slight (involving only a shifting of the direction of gaze a few degrees, from the eyes to an ear), its effects are explosive. The conversation is disrupted almost instantaneously. In some cases, the subject of this experiment will seek to save the situation by rotating to bring his eyes into your line of gaze; if you continue to gaze at his ear, he may rotate through a full 360 degrees. Most often, however, the conversation is irretrievably damaged. Shock, anger, and vertigo are experienced not only by the "victim" but, oddly enough, by the experimenter himself. It is virtually impossible for

Reprinted from the *Schizophrenia Bulletin,* 1 (Fall, 1970), 15–20.

either party to sustain the conversation, or even to think coherently, as long as the experiment continues.

The point of this experiment is to suggest the presence of a public order that is all-pervasive, yet taken almost completely for granted. During the simplest kinds of public encounter, there are myriad understandings about comportment that govern the participants' behavior—understandings governing posture, facial expression, and gestures, as well as the content and form of the language used. In speech itself, the types of conformity are extremely diverse and include pronunciation; grammar and syntax; loudness, pitch, and phrasing; and aspiration. Almost all of these elements are so taken for granted that they "go without saying" and are more or less invisible, not only to the speakers but to society at large. These understandings constitute part of our society's assumptive world, the world that is thought of as normal, decent, and possible.

The probability that these understandings are, for the most part, arbitrary to a particular historical culture (is shaking hands or rubbing noses a better form of greeting?) is immaterial to the individual member of society whose attitude of everyday life is, *whatever is, is right.* There is a social, cultural, and interpersonal status quo whose existence is felt only when abrogated. Since violations occur infrequently, and since the culture provides no very adequate vocabulary for talking about either the presence or abuse of its invisible understandings, such deviations are considered disruptive and disturbing. The society member's loyalty to his culture's unstated conventions is unthinking but extremely intense.

The sociologist Mannheim referred to such intense and unconscious loyalty to the status quo as *ideological.* Ideology, in this sense, refers not only to the defense of explicit political or economic interests but, much more broadly, to a whole world view or perspective on what reality is. As a contrast to the ideological view, Mannheim cited the *utopian* outlook, which tends "to shatter, either partially or wholly, the order of things prevailing at the time." [1] The attitude of everyday life, which is ideological, is transfixed by the past and the present; the possibility of a radically different scheme of things, or revolutionary changes in custom and outlook, is thereby rejected. The utopian perspective, by contrast, is fixed on the future; it rejects the status quo with abrupt finality. *Social change* arises out of the clash of the ideological and utopian perspectives.

RESIDUAL RULE VIOLATIONS

It is the thesis of this paper that the concepts of mental illness in general—and schizophrenia in particular—are not neutral, value-free,

---

[1] Mannheim, K. *Ideology and Utopia.* London: Routledge and Kegan, 1936.

scientifically precise terms but are, for the most part, the leading edge of an ideology embedded in the historical and cultural present of the white middle class of Western societies. The concept of illness and its associated vocabulary—symptoms, therapies, patients, and physicians—reify and legitimate the prevailing public order at the expense of other possible worlds. The medical model of disease refers to culture-free processes that are independent of the public order; a case of pneumonia or syphilis is pretty much the same in New York or New Caledonia.[2]

Most of the "symptoms" of mental illness, however, are of an entirely different nature. Far from being culture-free, such "symptoms" are themselves offenses against implicit understandings of particular cultures. Every society provides its members with a set of explicit norms—understandings governing conduct with regard to such central institutions as the state, the family, and private property. Offenses against these norms have conventional names; for example, an offense against property is called "theft," and an offense against sexual propriety is called "perversion." As we have seen above, however, the public order also is made up of countless unnamed understandings. "Everyone knows," for example, that during a conversation one looks at the other's eyes or mouth, but not at his ear. For the convenience of the society, offenses against these unnamed residual understandings are usually lumped together in a miscellaneous, catchall category. If people reacting to an offense exhaust the conventional categories that might define it (e.g., theft, prostitution, and drunkenness), yet are certain that an offense has been committed, they may resort to this residual category. In earlier societies, the residual category was witchcraft, spirit possession, or possession by the devil; today, it is mental illness. The symptoms of mental illness are, therefore, violations of residual rules.

To be sure, some residual-rule violations are expressions of underlying physiological processes: the hallucinations of the toxic psychoses and the delusions associated with general paresis, for example. Perhaps future research will identify further physiological processes that lead to violations of residual rules. For the present, however, the key attributes of the medical model have yet to be established and verified for the major mental illnesses. There has been no scientific verification of the cause, course, site of pathology, uniform and invariant signs and symptoms, and treatment of choice for almost all the conventional, "functional" diagnostic categories. Psychiatric knowledge in these matters rests almost entirely on unsystematic clinical impressions and professional lore. It is quite possible, therefore,

[2] For criticisms of the medical model, see Goffman, E. *Asylums*. New York: Doubleday-Anchor, 1961; Laing, R. *The Politics of Experience*. New York: Pantheon, 1967; Lemert, E. M. *Social Pathology*. New York: McGraw-Hill, 1951; Scheff, Thomas, J. *Being Mentally Ill: A Sociological Theory*. Chicago: Aldine, 1966; Szasz, T. S. *The Myth of Mental Illness*. New York: Hoeber-Harper, 1961; Ullman, L. P., and Krasner, L. *A Psychological Approach to Abnormal Behavior*. Englewood Cliffs, N.J.: Prentice-Hall, 1969.

that many psychiatrists' and other mental-health workers' "absolute certainty" about the cause, site, course, symptoms, and treatment of mental illness represents an ideological reflex, a spirited defense of the present social order.

RESIDUE OF RESIDUES

Viewed as offenses against the public order, the symptoms of schizophrenia are particularly interesting. Of all the major diagnostic categories, the concept of schizophrenia (although widely used by psychiatrists in the United States and in those countries influenced by American psychiatric nomenclature) is the vaguest and least clearly defined. Such categories as obsession, depression, and mania at least have a vernacular meaning. Schizophrenia, however, is a broad gloss; it involves, in no very clear relationship, ideas such as "inappropriateness of affect," "impoverishment of thought," "inability to be involved in meaningful human relationships," "bizarre behavior" (such as delusions and hallucinations), "disorder of speech and communication," and "withdrawal."

These very broadly defined symptoms can be redefined as offenses against implicit social understandings. The appropriateness of emotional expression is, after all, a cultural judgment. Grief is deemed appropriate in our society at a funeral, but not at a party. In other cultures, however, such judgments of propriety may be reversed. With regard to thought disorder, cultural anthropologists have long been at pains to point out that ways of thought are fundamentally different in different societies. What constitutes a meaningful human relationship, anthropologists also report, is basically different in other times and places. Likewise, behavior that is bizarre in one culture is deemed tolerable or even necessary in another. Disorders of speech and communication, again, can be seen as offenses against culturally prescribed rules of language and expression. Finally, the notion of "withdrawal" assumes a cultural standard concerning the degree of involvement and the amount of distance between the individual and those around him.

The broadness and vagueness of the concept of schizophrenia suggest that it may serve as the residue of residues. As diagnostic categories such as hysteria and depression have become conventionalized names for residual rule breaking, a need seems to have developed for a still more generalized, miscellaneous diagnostic category. If this is true, the schizophrenic explores not only "inner space" (Ronald Laing's phrase) but also the normative boundaries of his society.

These remarks should not be taken to suggest that there is no internal experience associated with "symptomatic" behavior; the individual with symptoms *does* experience distress and suffering, or under some conditions, exhilaration and freedom. The point is, however, that public, consensual "knowledge" of mental illness is based, by and large, on knowledge not of these internal states but of their overt manifestations. When a person runs down the street naked and screaming, lay and professional diagnosticians alike assume the existence of mental illness within that person—even though they have not investigated his internal state. Mental-health procedure and the conceptual apparatus of the medical model posit internal states, but the events actually observed are external.

LABELING THEORY

A point of view that is an alternative to the medical model, and that acknowledges the culture-bound nature of mental illness, is afforded by labeling theory in sociology.[3] Like the evidence supporting the medical model, which is uneven and in large measure unreliable, the body of knowledge in support of the labeling theory of mental illness is by no means weighty or complete enough to prove its correctness.[4] But even though labeling theory is hypothetical, its use may afford perspective—if only because it offers a viewpoint that, along a number of different dimensions, is diametrically opposed to the medical model.

The labeling theory of deviance, when applied to mental illness, may be presented as a series of nine hypotheses:[5]

1. Residual rule breaking arises from fundamentally diverse sources (that is, organic, psychological, situations of stress, volitional acts of innovation or defiance).

2. Relative to the rate of treated mental illness, the rate of unrecorded residual rule breaking is extremely high.

3. Most residual rule breaking is "denied" and is of transitory significance.

4. Stereotyped imagery of mental disorder is learned in early childhood.

5. The stereotypes of insanity are continually reaffirmed, inadvertently, in ordinary social interaction.

6. Labeled deviants may be rewarded for playing the stereotyped deviant role.

7. Labeled deviants are punished when they attempt to return to conventional roles.

[3] For a general statement of labeling theory, see Becker, H. *Outsiders.* New York: Free Press, 1963.

[4] Supporting evidence can be found in Balint, M. *The Doctor, the Patient, and the Illness.* New York: International Universities Press, 1957; Laing, R., and Esterson, A. *Sanity, Madness and the Family.* London: Tavistock, 1964; Lemert, E. M. *Social Pathology.* New York: McGraw-Hill, 1951; Scheff, Thomas J. *Mental Illness and Social Processes.* New York: Harper & Row, 1967; Spitzer, S. P., and Denzin, N. K. *The Mental Patient: Studies in the Sociology of Deviance.* New York: McGraw-Hill, 1968.

[5] Scheff, Thomas J. *Being Mentally Ill: A Sociological Theory.* Chicago: Aldine, 1966.

8. In the crisis occurring when a residual rule breaker is publicly labeled, the deviant is highly suggestible and may accept the label.

9. Among residual rule breakers, labeling is the single most important cause of careers of residual deviance.

According to labeling theory, the societal reaction is the key process that determines outcome in most cases of residual rule breaking. That reaction may be either denial (the most frequent reaction) or labeling. Denial is to "normalize" the rule breaking by ignoring or rationalizing it ("boys will be boys"). The key hypothesis in labeling theory is that when residual rule breaking is denied, the rule breaking will generally be transitory (as when the stress causing rule breaking is removed: e.g., the cessation of sleep deprivation), compensated for, or channeled into some socially acceptable form. If, however, labeling occurs (that is, if the rule breaker is segregated as a stigmatized deviant), the rule breaking that would otherwise have been terminated, compensated for, or channeled may be stabilized; thus, the offender, through the agency of labeling, is launched on a career of "chronic mental illness." Crucial to the production of chronicity, therefore, are the contingencies (often external to the deviants) that give rise to labeling rather than denial: for instance, the visibility of the rule breaking, the power of the rule breaker relative to persons reacting to his behavior, the tolerance level of the community, and the availability in the culture of alternative channels of response other than labeling (among Indian tribes, for example, involuntary trance states may be seen as a qualification for a desirable position in the society, such as that of shaman).

"SCHIZOPHRENIA"—A LABEL

On the basis of the foregoing discussion, it seems likely that labeling theory would prove particularly strategic in investigating schizophrenia. Schizophrenia is the single most widely used diagnosis for mental illness in the United States, yet the cause, site, course, and treatment of choice are unknown, or are subjects of heated and voluminous controversy. Moreover, there is some evidence that the reliability of diagnosis of schizophrenia is quite low. Finally, there is little agreement on whether a disease entity of schizophrenia even exists, what constitutes schizophrenia's basic signs and symptoms if it *does* exist, and how these symptoms are to be reliably and positively identified in the diagnostic process. Because of the all but overwhelming uncertainties and ambiguities inherent in its definition, "schizophrenia" is an appellation, or "label," which may be easily applied to those residual rule breakers whose deviant behavior is difficult to classify.

In this connection, it is interesting to note the enormous anomaly of classification procedures in most schizophrenia research. The hypothetical cause of schizophrenia, the independent variable in the research design—whether it is a physiological, biochemical, or psychological attribute—is measured with considerable attention to reliability, validity, and precision. I have seen reports of biochemical research in which the independent variable is measured to two decimal places. Yet the measurement of the dependent variable, the diagnosis of schizophrenia, is virtually ignored. Obviously, the precision of the measurement is virtually nil, since it represents at best an ordinal scale, or, much more likely, a nominal scale. In most studies, the reliability and validity of the diagnosis receives no attention at all: an experimental group is assembled by virtue of hospital diagnoses—leaving the measurement of the dependent variable to the mercy of the obscure vagaries of the process of psychiatric screening and diagnosis. Labeling theory should serve at least to make this anomaly visible to researchers in the field of schizophrenia.

More broadly, the clash between labeling theory and the medical and psychological models of mental illness may serve to alert researchers to some of the fundamental assumptions that they may be making in setting up their research. Particular reference should be made to the question of whether they are unknowingly aligning themselves with the social status quo; for example, by accepting unexamined the diagnosis of schizophrenia, they may be inadvertently providing the legitimacy of science to what is basically a social value judgment. In the remainder of this chapter I wish to pursue this point—the part that medical science may be playing in legitimating the status quo.

As I indicated earlier, in social interaction there is a public order that is continually reaffirmed. Each time a member of the society conforms to the stated or unstated cultural expectations of that society, as when he gazes at the eyes of the person with whom he is conversing, he helps maintain the social status quo. Any deviation from these expectations, however small and regardless of its motivation, may be a threat to the status quo, since most social change occurs through the gradual erosion of custom.

Since all social orders are, as far as we know, basically arbitrary, a threat to society's fundamental customs impels its conforming members to look to extrasocial sources of legitimacy for the status quo. In societies completely under the sway of a single, monolithic religion, the source of legitimacy is always supernatural. Thus, during the Middle Ages the legitimacy of the social order was maintained by reference to God's commands, as found in the Bible and interpreted by the Catholic Church. The Pope was God's deputy, the kings ruled by divine right, the particular cultural form that the family happened to take at the time—the patrilocal, monogamous, nuclear family—was sanctified by the church, and so on.

In modern societies, however, it is increasingly difficult to base legitimacy upon appeals to supernatural sources. As complete, unquestioning religious faith has weakened, one very important new source of legitimacy has emerged: in the eyes of laymen, modern science offers the kind of absolute certainty once provided by the church. The institution of medicine is in a particularly strategic position in this regard, because the physician is the only representative of science with whom the average man associates. To the extent that medical science lends its name to the labeling of nonconformity as mental illness, it is giving legitimacy to the social status quo. The mental-health researcher may protest that he is interested not in the preservation of the status quo but in a scientific question: "What are the causes of mental illness?" According to the argument given here, however, his question is loaded—as is "When did you stop beating your wife?" or, more to the point, "What are the causes of witchcraft?" [6] Thus, a question about causality may also be ideological, in Mannheim's sense, in that it reaffirms current social beliefs, if only inadvertently.

2

ON REASON AND SANITY: SOME POLITICAL IMPLICATIONS OF PSYCHIATRIC THOUGHT
Thomas J. Scheff

Chapter 2 uses labeling theory as a basis for exploring some of the broader implications of the medical model of mental illness. The discussion continues, and explores in somewhat greater detail, the analysis that was begun in Chapter 1—that the medical model, when applied to the phenomenon labeled mental illness, may have an ideological function; that is, it may help to reaffirm the current cultural, and thereby the political, status quo in our society. Since this chapter was written in the late 60's, the political context is no longer exactly the same as it was. For

Reprinted from Transcultural Research in Mental Health, Volume II of Mental Health Research in Asia and the Pacific, William P. Lebra (Ed.), The University Press of Hawaii: Honolulu, 1972, pp. 400–407.

[6] Szasz, T. S. *The Manufacture of Madness.* New York: Harper & Row, 1970.

example, there has been a partial U.S. withdrawal from Indo-China. I would maintain, however, that the underlying political context is sufficiently similar so that the argument still applies.

About seventy-five years ago a psychologist named Stratton conducted a series of excellent studies of the individual's perceptual world.[1] His procedure was unusual but simple: he designed a pair of prismatic spectacles, which inverted his field of vision. He wore these glasses during all his waking hours for several periods of many weeks. One of his findings, as might be expected, was that the experience, at least initially, was almost totally disorienting. The inversion of up and down destroyed his customary world, so that even the most trivial activity, such as tying his shoelaces, was nearly impossible.

It can be argued that the individual's experience is mediated by a whole series of absolute dimensions, which give him a sense of continuity, mastery, and agency in his endeavors. Some of the dimensions are physical, such as up and down, left and right, the geographic sense of location in space, the temporal or historic sense of location in time (with respect to a calendar, say). Some of these axes are not physical, but social and/or psychological. In a racist society, for example, the axis of racial separation is probably one such absolute dimension. Any perturbation along this axis is perceived by the members of the society as a cataclysmic dislocation, with the concomitant feelings of vertigo, nausea, and paralysis. In such a society, the worth and value of a white man and his sense of self-esteem is constantly witnessed and affirmed by his sense of the inferiority of the black. The racial axis allows him to locate himself, not in physical time and space, but in social time and in moral space.

In an experiment somewhat analogous to Stratton's, a white man, Griffin, changed the color of his skin and became a "Negro." [2] Like Stratton, he experienced almost total disorientation. An interesting difference between the two studies, however, was that Griffin's experience proved to be irreversible. He was thrown out of orbit, so to speak. When Stratton took off the glasses, he returned to his customary place in his society, an ordinary man among men. But Griffin's experiment so perturbed his position in the society that he found himself unable to return to his customary place.

In modern mass societies there are probably many other important absolute axes, such as nationality and ideology. Particularly in the United States, the capitalist-communist axis and the closely related axis of nationalism that separates Americans from aliens probably operate like

[1] George M. Stratton, "Some Preliminary Experiments on Vision Without Inversion of the Retinal Image," *Psychological Review* 3 (1897), 611–17; and "Vision Without Inversion of the Retinal Image," *Psychological Review* 4 (1897), 463–81.

[2] John Howard Griffin, *Black Like Me* (New York: Signet, 1960).

the racial axis discussed above. All three of these axes are similar psychologically in that they identify an in-group—the white American, "free enterprise" population—at the expense of out-groups—the blacks, the communists, and the aliens.

There is another, more subtle axis of contemporary experience, which because it is more pervasive is even more important than those already mentioned. This is the axis of reason and unreason, rationality and irrationality, or, most relevant to our discussion here, the related axis of sanity and insanity, which in its most contemporary guise is the axis of mental health and mental illness. In a richly detailed account, Foucault has shown how the successive concepts of madness in the last four hundred years of European history paralleled and reflected the successive conceptions of reason.[3] Although Foucault's narrative is labyrinthine, it gives a marvelously embroidered description of the relationship between the ethos and the handling of the "insane." For our present purposes, it makes this central point: conceptions and practices regarding insanity relate intimately to and influence contemporary sensibilities concerning reason and rationality.

In this chapter, I wish to make two points. First, the dimension of mental health and mental illness is not an absolute fact of nature, like the physical directions of up and down, but a moral axis, like the social separation of whites and blacks. Second, the confusion of the absolute and social bases in the distinction between sanity and insanity has political consequences. I will first discuss the cultural arbitrariness of contemporary concepts of sanity and insanity.

Although most researchers in the area of mental illness speak with assurance about diagnostic entities such as schizophrenia, the scientific basis for these classifications remains obscure at best. For the major mental illness classifications, none of the components of the medical model has been demonstrated: cause, lesion, uniform and invariate symptoms, course, and treatment of choice.[4] Studies of the reliability of psychiatric diagnosis show the levels to be low. Even at the theoretical level, there is little consensus about the nature of these diseases, *vide* the concepts of schizophrenia and sociopathy.

In the areas of positive mental health, the confusion is even more apparent. In a recent view of concepts of mental health, Jahoda found six competing concepts:

1. Mastery of the environment
2. Self-actualization
3. Self-esteem
4. Integration of self

[3] Michel Foucault, *Madness and Civilization* (New York: Mentor, 1967).
[4] T. J. Scheff, *Being Mentally Ill* (Chicago: Aldine, 1966).

5. Autonomy

6. Adequacy of perception of reality[5]

The prospect of choosing between these six different criteria, as advanced by different experts, is disquieting enough. When one notes that some of 'the criteria may be contradictory (for example, mastery of the environment versus self-actualization, and perception of reality versus autonomy) and that none has been operationally defined or investigated, one begins to perceive the state of chaos that characterizes the concept from a scientific point of view. It appears that mental health is not a physical fact, but a value choice about what kind of men we *should* be and what kinds of values we should encourage in our society. Whether one selects a notion such as aggressive mastery of the environment, traditionally a Western ideal, or the more inward-turning goal of self-actualization, which is more akin to traditional ideals in the Orient, is not dictated by the natural order of stably reoccurring regularities in nature, but by human choice.

Just as mental health may be seen as a value choice about how men should behave, so the symptoms of mental illness can be seen as value choices about how men should not behave. Thought and behavior that are taken to be correct in each culture are so taken for granted that the assumptions of propriety are largely invisible to its members. If one goes to the local cafeteria and butts in at the head of the line, there would be a reaction from those standing in line. If the intruder asked what the trouble was, he would be told, "First come, first served," or something similar. Suppose, however, he continued in line and decided not to carry his own tray for his food but to place his food on the tray of the stranger behind him. He might be told that in this cafeteria one carries one's own tray. More likely, because "everybody knows" that, he might be eyed with suspicion and alarm. Continuing the example, suppose that after sitting down with the stranger, he notices some food on his plate that looks particularly tempting. He reaches across the table, spearing some of the food with his fork. This action, although it is no more than the violation of custom, would probably place the offender beyond the pale.

There are literally myriad customs associated with each culture that "go without saying," to the point that violations leave the conforming member of the society baffled. His society has not prepared him for violations; they exist outside his vocabulary of motives. In speaking even simple sentences, there are thousands of understandings about proper grammar, syntax, pitch, loudness, rhythm, gesture, and so forth, that are part of any living language. The most elementary conversation is embedded in a whole network of understandings about comportment. For example, there is a

[5] Marie Jahoda, *Current Concepts of Positive Mental Health* (New York: Basic Books, 1958).

conversational distance, neither too far, nor too close. When one speaks, one looks in certain directions: at the hearer's eyes or mouth, but not at his ear or forehead. Breaking so simple a custom results in the most violent kind of reaction.

Although the reaction to violation of customs such as the ones discussed here is violent and complete, it must be remembered that these customs are largely conventions in a particular culture, and as such are for the most part arbitrary and subject to change and transformation. They are not absolute, sacred, or immutable.

Foucault traces the confusion of values and science in modern psychiatry from its beginning in the nineteenth century:

> As positivism imposes itself upon medicine and psychiatry, this practice becomes more and more obscure, the psychiatrist's powers more and more miraculous, and the doctor-patient couple sinks deeper into a strange world. In the patient's eyes, the doctor becomes a thaumaturge; the authority he has borrowed from order, morality, and the family now seems to derive from himself; it is because he is a doctor that he is believed to possess these powers, and while Pinel, with Tuke, strongly asserted that his moral action was not necessarily linked to any scientific competence, it was thought, and by the patient first of all, that it was in the esotericism of his knowledge, in some almost daemonic secret of knowledge, that the doctor had found the power to unravel insanity.[6]

It need hardly be mentioned that the "order, morality, and the family" from which psychiatrists "borrowed" authority are the order, morality, and family structure of a particular society, and therefore do not constitute absolute axes.

But in the everyday life of the members of the society, these axes are seen as absolute, and therefore as sacred and immutable. In a study somewhat akin to those of Stratton and Griffin, Goffman wandered the halls of St. Elizabeth's hospital. Dressed shabbily, he was usually taken to be a patient. His statement gathers some of its impact from the reversal of the dimension of the sane and the insane: in his analysis, he identifies with the patients; most of his narrative is from their point of view.[7] Readers of *Asylums* report some of the reactions that occur when an axis that is assumed to be absolute is reversed: fear, fury, and awe.

From my own studies of commitment proceedings and from subsequent confirmation of these studies by others, it seems that the separation of the members of a society along the axis of sanity and insanity is largely a product of social rather than medical or scientific selection. Virtually all persons who are proposed by members of the community (or by public agencies such as the police) are accepted for treatment. The medical "examinations" that supposedly determine whether the candidate is sane

---

[6] Foucault, *Madness and Civilization*, p. 220.
[7] Erving Goffman, *Asylums* (Garden City, N.Y.: Doubleday-Anchor, 1961).

or insane are, as a rule, peremptory and ritualistic. The actual goal in most of these examinations, and this includes the various diagnostic evaluations in the hospital also, seems not to be *whether* the candidate is mentally ill, but *which* mental illness he has.[8] Like the separation of blacks and whites, the sorting of the insane from the sane is primarily a social fact and not a fact of nature. Human beings have literally hundreds of physical attributes that are as visible as skin color: height, weight, attractiveness, and so on. That skin color is the criterion of separation is a social choice rather than the inevitable product of physical processes that lie outside of human control, as upholders of racist societies would have us believe. Similarly, the segregation of the "mentally ill" is also a product of social choice, rather than the ineluctable product of genetic, biochemical, or psychodynamic processes, as the upholders of the psychiatric status quo would have us believe.

Let us now turn to the so-called mental illnesses, such as schizophrenia. There are two major issues here. The first deals with the question of the existence of a behavioral system, an entity that is referred to as schizophrenia. As indicated above, the scientific basis for this label is unclear. The second point is to some degree independent of the first. Even if it were granted that there were such a system, would it necessarily follow that the energies of reasonable men be directed toward finding, analyzing, and changing such behavior? According to the concept of schizophrenia that is held by some psychiatrists, the attributes of schizophrenia are withdrawal, flatness of affect, thought disorder, language aberrations, and hallucinations or delusions. The schizophrenic is pictured, therefore, as a passive, inward-dwelling, remote person who lacks interpersonal and other competences that other members of the society see as necessary to maintain or improve one's status in society. Although these symptoms are stated in such a way as to suggest that

[8] Mechanic reported that the two hospitals he studied (in California) accepted all patients; David Mechanic, "Some Factors in Identifying and Defining Mental Illness," *Mental Hygiene* 46 (1962), 66–74. My own systematic studies of the rates of acceptance and the thoroughness of the psychiatric examinations were conducted in Wisconsin, and reported in *Being Mentally Ill* (see note 4 above). Independent replication (in California) of my findings is found in the report by the Petris Committee of the Legislature of the State of California: *The Dilemma of Mental Commitments in California*, Final Report, 1967. As a result of these findings, a new law, which substantially changes commitment and other proceedings (the Lanterman-Petris-Short law), went into effect on June 1, 1969 in California.

It is interesting to note that in England reviewers of *Being Mentally Ill* accept these findings, which they take to demonstrate the inferiority of American psychiatry. They seem to take for granted, without any evidence, that English hospitals are more discriminating and English psychiatric examinations more thorough. The evidence I collected in an English psychiatric hospital in London contradicts this assumption. As far as I could tell, the rates of acceptance and the level of thoroughness there were identical to those I reported in the United States. For my summary report, see "Hospitalization of the Mentally Ill in Italy, England, and the United States," *American Philosophical Society, Yearbook*, 1966, pp. 523–24.

they are in some way deviations from absolute and immutable standards, this is not necessarily the case. Withdrawal may be considered a violation of customary expectations about the degree of social and interpersonal distance that is held in the society, and flatness of affect, a violation of expectations about expressive gestures. The language aberrations can obviously be seen as transgressions, not against the rules of nature, but of language, which are, of course, arbitrary. What about thought disorder and hallucinations and delusions? It has already been suggested that there are culturally derived rules about propriety. Similarly, it is suggested that there are culture-bound rules about thought and about reality. To illustrate rules about reality, consider the effort Western parents go through to convince their children that dreams and nightmares are not real, but that disease germs are real. The child has seen and experienced nightmares but has never seen germs. After some struggle, the parents convince him. But in some traditional societies the scheme is reversed: the dreams are real, and the germs are not.

Not only are the expectations that lead to the absolute rejection of "schizophrenic symptoms" arbitrary; it may be argued that the evaluation of conventional sanity as desirable and of "mental disease," such as schizophrenia, as undesirable should be reversed. According to the conventional picture of schizophrenics, they would not have the competence or the motivation to napalm civilians, defoliate forests and rice crops, and to push the button that would destroy much of the world that we know. These activities are carried out by persons sane by conventional definition, and encouraged, or at least not discouraged, by the great majority of the "sane" people in the society.

A few years ago, Senator Richard Russell of Georgia, head of the Armed Services Committee of the Senate and a few years ago one of the three or four most powerful men in the U.S., said: "If we have to start over again with another Adam and Eve, I want them to be Americans; and I want them on this continent and not in Europe." Senator Russell's liberty will not be removed because of that statement: his speech is coherent, there was no evidence of delusions or hallucinations, his affect was appropriate to his patriotic sentiments, and there was no indication of thought disorder. His calm willingness to see virtually all of the three billion people on earth sacrificed to his notion of patriotism does not raise questions about his sanity, as long as we continue to use conventional ideas about sanity. The current definitions of insanity leave men like Senator Russell at large and with the power to snuff out life on this planet.

As many of the current discussions regarding "preventive detention" make clear, there is often great difficulty in predicting the dangerousness of a person from his history, actions, or statements. Persons who make threatening statements often do not carry them out. On the other hand, persons without any violence in their record have, on occasion, become murderers. The prediction of dangerous actions from past behavior is not a highly developed science. Even granting this, however, surely Russell's statement must stand as one of the most threatening ever made. A society in which there were even a little prudence would surely take steps, such as "preventive detention," to see that a man with Russell's ideas and power not be allowed to continue in a position where he might help put an end to the human race.

Current definitions of insanity mobilize society to locate, segregate, and "treat" schizophrenics and other persons who are "out of touch with reality." Perhaps the time has come to consider the possibility that the reality that the so-called schizophrenics are out of touch with is so appalling that their view of the world may be more supportive to life than conventional reality.

I am not suggesting that Richard Russell is insane, but that the contemporary vision of sanity and reason is arbitrary and distorted. Current notions of psychiatry and mental health bring to the present crisis of human experience stereotypes of danger and threat that make us ill-equipped to respond. By mobilizing the energies and sensibilities of our society to act against schizophrenics, on the one hand, and remaining silent about the erosion of reason among the respectable leaders and their followers in the larger society, on the other hand, psychiatric practice and research condones the status quo.

The implicit support given the sttus quo by current psychiatric concepts and practice is especially important, because the man in the street takes psychiatry to be a scientific enterprise. To the extent that practitioners and researchers in the field of mental illness argue and act as if mental illness is largely a technical, scientific issue rather than an area that is almost completely governed by moral values, they are functioning as accomplices to the current moral status quo. It is always tempting for the scientist to take the easiest way, which is to treat his job as exclusively concerned with means rather than ends. This bureaucratization of science demeans the scientist to a mere technician, and induces him to avoid his responsibilities as an intellectual and citizen.

To become worthy of his power the scientist will need to develop enough wisdom and humane understanding to recognize that the acquisition of knowledge is intricately interwoven with the pursuit of goals. It has often been pointed out that the nineteenth century slogan, "Survival of the fittest," begged the question because it did not state what fitness was for. Likewise, it is not possible to plan man's future without deciding beforehand what he should be fitted for, in other words, what human destiny ought to be—a decision loaded with ethical values. What is new is not necessarily good, and all changes, even those apparently the most desirable, are always fraught with unpredictable consequences. The scientist must beware of having to admit, like Captain Ahab in Melville's *Moby Dick*, "All my means are sane; my motives and objects mad." [9]

I am also not suggesting that psychiatrists and other workers in the field of mental illness are more at fault than the rest of the society. As it becomes increasingly evident that the United States is committed to overt dominion in Asia, and covert counterrevolutionary manipulation in the rest of the world, virtually all of the segments of American society fall into place, either by acts of commission or omission.[10] What Conor Cruise O'Brien has called the "counterrevolutionary subordination" of science and scholarship has been proceeding apace for the last twenty years. Many social scientists are directly involved in the planning of brutal and inhuman procedures to be used by the military, for example, the "population control" programs in Vietnam. Other scholars, though not directly involved, approve the steps taken. Still others, and this includes most of the foremost scholars, conduct their work in such a way that objective scholarship is suborned to the interests of American power.[11]

What I am suggesting is that researchers in the field of mental illness—to the extent that they follow contemporary social definitions of sanity and insanity, reason and unreason, without question or investigation—are helping to further confound the moral issues by giving laymen the impression, however subtly or unintentionally, that there is absolute scientific justification for the prevailing American world view. It is our responsibility as scholars and students of human behavior to make visible the hidden moral values in psychiatry and mental health, so that they can be made the subject of research and open public discussion. Only in this way will we have borne witness as scientists and scholars in contributing our knowledge of human affairs to the area of politics. With patience and ingenuity, it should be possible to make the invisible visible. The enterprise I have in mind is not a small one; it is to explore and help recreate current concepts of sanity in particular and, more broadly, of reason and rationality.

[9] Rene Dubos, *Mirage of Health: Utopias, Progress, and Biological Change* (New York: Harper & Row, 1959), pp. 229–30.

[10] Neal D. Houghton (editor), *Struggle Against History: U.S. Foreign Policy in an Age of Revolution* (New York: Simon & Schuster, 1968).

[11] Noam Chomsky, *American Power and the New Mandarins* (New York: Pantheon, 1969). This paragraph was written in 1969, when American war on Asia was reaching its peak. Although overt American counter-revolutionary actions have receded during the last two years, there is no sign that the basic policy has changed. For example, in a recent (September, 1974) Associated Press report, it was indicated that the United States is currently providing military and economic support for 56 dictatorial and authoritarian governments.

3

THE LABELING THEORY
OF MENTAL ILLNESS
Thomas J. Scheff

The emphasis in Chapter 3 changes from the ideological implications of labeling theory, which has been the concern of Chapters 1 and 2, to its scientific implications. This chapter first reviews and responds to criticisms of labeling theory. It then assesses the state of evidence regarding the theory, by reviewing those studies that may be used to determine its validity.

This chapter evaluates the labeling theory of mental illness. To date, there have been three critiques of labeling theory, those by Gove (1970a), Gibbs (1972), and Davis (1972). Gibbs and Davis, for the most part, evaluate formal aspects of the theory; Gove evaluates its substance. Gibbs suggests that the labeling approach is not really a scientific theory in that it is not sufficiently explicit and unambiguous. Davis proposes that there are ideological biases in the labeling approach, and points to alternative approaches.[1]

Although the papers by Gibbs and by Davis raise important questions, neither considers at length the most fundamental question that can be asked about a theory: how well is it supported by empirical studies? Gove considers this question in his critique, and the present chapter is devoted to it, also. In the first section of this chapter I will respond to Gove's evaluation, and in the second, present my own.

First, however, I wish to comment on Gibbs's paper, for it raises a methodological question relevant to assessing the evidence to be presented below. In his analysis of labeling theory, Gibbs demonstrates that the concepts used in the theory are ambiguous because they are not defined denotatively—that is, in a way that allows only a single meaning for each

Reprinted, with slight modifications, from the *American Sociological Review*, 39 (June, 1974), 444–52.

I wish to acknowledge the helpful advice of Norman Denzin, James Greenley, C. Allen Haney, Arnold Linsky, and William Rushing, who read an earlier draft of this chapter.

[1] For a considered response to the question of bias in labeling theory, see Becker (1973).

concept. He argues that this ambiguity leaves open many alternative meanings and implications. For this reason, he concludes that the theory in its present state is of little value.

I will make two observations about Gibbs's argument. First, virtually every other sociological theory lacks denotative definition. Indeed, Gibbs observes that the concept of social norm, an important element in labeling theory, has never been defined denotatively. Inasmuch as this concept is perhaps the basic sociological concept, Gibbs's critique is less an evaluation of labeling theory per se than of the state of social science.

Note that Gibbs's critique is equally applicable to psychiatric theories. At this writing, I know of no psychiatric theory of functional mental illness that is based on denotatively defined concepts. As applied to mental illness, the four basic components of the medical model—cause, lesion, symptoms, and outcome—are not defined denotatively (Scheff, 1966: 180). Nor are such specific concepts as depression, schizophrenia, phobia, and neurosis. Gibbs's critique of labeling theory, therefore, applies equally well to all of the competing theories in the field of mental illness.

My second observation is that Gibbs's critique implies that there is only one kind of science, a positivistic one modeled on natural science. He appears to be saying that a theory has no value unless it can be stated unambiguously. It has been argued, however, that concepts and theories can have a sensitizing function quite distinct from their truth value (Blumer, 1954). Theories based on nominal (connotative) definitions can direct attention toward new data or to new ways of perceiving old data, which challenge taken-for-granted assumptions and shatter "the attitude of everyday life" (Bruyn, 1966; Schutz, 1962). According to such a view, the very ambiguousness of nominal concepts is of value, for these concepts have a rich evocativeness that denotative concepts lack (Bronowski, 1965).

Science may be viewed as a problem-solving activity with two distinct phases (Bronowski, 1956). In the first phase, the problem is to somehow transcend the traditional classifications and models that imprison thought. In the second, the problem is to test a new idea meticulously. Sensitizing theories are relevant to the first phase of scientific problem solving. They are attempts to jostle the imagination, to create a crisis of consciousness that will lead to new visions of reality. Sensitizing theories are as valuable as denotative theories; they simply attempt to solve a different problem.

The need for new research directions in the study of mental illness has long been apparent. Although thousands of studies have been based on the medical model, real progress toward scientific understanding, or even a fruitful formulation of the problem, is lacking (Scheff, 1966: 7-9). The sensitizing function of the labeling theory of mental illness derives precisely from its attempt to contradict the major tenets of the medical model; it is less an attempt to displace that model than to clear the air, as I indicated in *Being Mentally Ill*:

It should be clear at this point that the purpose of this theory is *not* to reject psychiatric and psychological formulations in their totality. It is obvious that such formulations have served, and will continue to serve, useful functions in theory and practice concerning mental illness. The . . . purpose, rather, is to develop a model which will complement the individual system models by providing a complete and explicit contrast. . . . By allowing for explicit consideration of these antithetical models, the way may be cleared for a synthesis. . . . (Scheff, 1966: 25–26, 27)

It seems to me that none of the three critiques cited above appreciate the point that a sensitizing theory may be ambiguous, ideologically biased, and not literally true, and may still be useful and even necessary for scientific progress.

Although the labeling theory of mental illness is a sensitizing theory, it can yet be used to evaluate evidence in a provisional way. The proper question to ask is not, as Gove asks, whether labeling theory is literally true, but whether the relevant studies are more consistent with labeling theory than with its competitor, the medical model. I will now turn to this question.

Gove's argument consists of two points. The first concerns entry into the role of mentally ill, the second concerns the consequences of hospitalization. Gove summarizes his position regarding the first point as follows:

The vast majority of persons who become patients have a serious disturbance, and it is only when the situation becomes untenable that action is taken. The public officials who perform the major screening role do not simply process all of the persons who come before them as mentally ill but instead screen out a large portion. If the person passes this initial screening, he will probably be committed, and there is reason to assume the process at this point frequently becomes somewhat ritualized. But even here a number of persons are released either through the psychiatric examination or the court hearing. (Gove, 1970a: 879)

Regarding the second point, Gove agrees that hospitalization may have debilitating consequences for the patient, but he argues that these may be outweighed by the following:

(1) There appear to be many restitutive processes associated with hospitalization. . . . (2) Patients treated in a modern psychiatric hospital typically do not spend enough time in the hospital to become truly institutionalized. (3) In most cases the stigma of having been a former mental patient does not appear to affect greatly one's performance in the community following discharge. (Gove 1970a: 882)

Gove reaches the following conclusion: "The available evidence . . . indicates that the societal reaction formulation of how a person becomes mentally ill is substantially incorrect" (1970a: 881). My own reading of the evidence is contrary to that of Gove. First, Gove's interpretation of most of the studies he cites seems at least questionable and in some cases inaccurate. Second, since Gove's articles were published, several new studies have appeared that are germane to the controversy. Also, Gove failed to mention several relevant articles that were published earlier than his article. I will review all of these articles later in this chapter. But first, I wish to state my objections to several of Gove's interpretations.

Gove's conclusion that the majority of the evidence failed to support labeling theory resulted from two kinds of distortion: first, Gove overstated the implications of those studies he thought refuted labeling theory, and, second, he misrepresented those studies he thought supported labeling theory. I will not try to refute all of Gove's interpretations, for to do so would be to restate labeling theory; I will simply indicate some representative errors that he makes.

Apropos of Gove's overstatement, let us examine how he interprets the study by Yarrow et al. (1955). To study the processes through which the next of kin come to define a person as mentally ill, Yarrow et al. interviewed wives of men who had been hospitalized for mental illness. Gove (1970a) summarizes that study as follows: "Only when the husband's behavior became impossible to deal with would the wife take action to have the husband hospitalized." Gove's interpretation is questionable for two reasons. First, Yarrow et al. studied only those cases of deviance that resulted in hospitalization. They did not study all cases, among the entire population, of each type of deviant behavior that led to hospitalization. The Yarrow et al. study thus covers only a clinical population, and is entirely ex post facto. Gove's interpretation repeats the classic fallacy of the medical model, which is to assume that hospitalization was inevitable, even though no observations were made on the incidence and outcome of similar cases in the unhospitalized population. The history of physical medicine has many analogous cases. For example, it has been found that until the late 1940s, histoplasmosis was thought to be a rare tropical disease with a uniformly fatal outcome (Schwartz and Baum, 1951). Field investigations discovered, however, that the syndrome is widely prevalent and that death or impairment is highly unusual. Analogously, it is possible that the symptoms reported by the wives in the Yarrow et al. study, even if accurately reported, might terminate without medical intervention.

The question of the accuracy of the wives' report raises the second problem in Gove's interpretation. Yarrow et al.'s descriptions of the husbands' behavior are based entirely on the wives' uncorroborated account. Yarrow et al. recognize this difficulty, warn the reader about it, and are unassuming about the implications of their findings:

Ideally to study this problem, one might like to interview the wives as they struggle with the developing illness. This is precluded, however, by the fact that the problem "is not visible" until psychiatric help is sought. The data, therefore, are the wives' reconstructions of their earlier experiences. . . . It is recognized that recollections of the prehospital period may well include systematic biases such as distortions, omissions, and increased organization and clarity. (Yarrow et al., 1955: 60)

Although Yarrow et al. clearly recognize the limitations of their study, Gove does not. He reports the wives' account of the husbands' behavior as if it were the thing itself. Judging from Gove, Laing and Esterson's (1964) detailed study of the way in which the next of kin sometimes falsifies his account and colludes against the prepatient may as well have never been written. Laing and Esterson spent an average of twenty-four hours interviewing members of each of the eleven families in their study, with a range of sixteen to fifty hours per family. They found considerable evidence in support of the patient's story rather than the next of kin's. For example, in one of their cases the psychiatrist indicated that the patient Maya had "ideas of reference," which supported one of the complaints against her. By interviewing the patient, the mother, and the father together, however, Laing and Esterson placed this "delusion" in a quite different light:

An idea of reference that she had was that something she could not fathom was going on between her parents, seemingly about her. Indeed there was. When they were interviewed together, her mother and father kept exchanging with each other a constant series of nods, winks, gestures, and knowing smiles so obvious to the observer that he commented on them after 20 minutes of the first such interview. They continued, however, unabated and denied. (Laing and Esterson, 1964: 24)

Laing and Esterson found many such items of misrepresentation by the next of kin in all their cases. Their study suggests that the uncorroborated account of the next of kin is riddled with error.

This is not to say that Laing and Esterson's interpretation is correct and that Gove's is not. I am saying that Yarrow et al.'s study and the other studies that Gove cites in this context were not only not organized to test labeling theory, but were innocent of any of the possible interpretations (such as that of Laing and Esterson) that labeling theory suggests. Until someone conducts systematic studies that investigate both clinical and nonclinical populations, and that do not rest entirely on the uncorroborated testimony of one or the other of the interested parties, interpretations of the kind that Gove makes are dubious.

Another example of how Gove distorts the evidence in seeking to discredit studies that support labeling theory is his analysis of my article, "The Societal Reaction to Deviance: Ascriptive Elements in the Psychiatric Screening of Mental Patients in a Midwestern State" (Scheff, 1964). The study reported in this article consisted of two phases. In the first, a preliminary phase, I had hospital psychiatrists rate a sample of incoming patients according to the legal criteria for commitment, dangerousness, and degree of mental impairment. In the second phase we observed, in a sample of cases, the procedures actually used in committing patients, particularly the psychiatric examination and the formal commitment hearing. The purpose of the psychiatric ratings was to provide a foundation for our observations in the second phase; the ratings were used to determine the extent to which there was any legal uncertainty about the patients' committability. The second phase of the study described how the judges and psychiatrists reacted to uncertainty. The article stated clearly that the study was divided into two parts:

The purpose of the description that follows is to determine the extent of uncertainty that exists concerning new patients' qualifications for involuntary confinement in a mental hospital, and the reactions of the courts to this type of uncertainty. (Scheff, 1964: 402)

In the first phase of the study, the psychiatrists' ratings of the sample of incoming patients were as follows:

DANGEROUSNESS

How Likely Patient Would Harm Self or Others		Degree of Mental Impairment	
Very likely	5%	Severe	17%
Likely	4%	Moderate	42%
Somewhat likely	14%	Mild	25%
Somewhat unlikely	20%	Minimal	12%
Unlikely	37%	None	2%
Very unlikely	18%		

I argued that these findings are relevant to the question of the legal uncertainty concerning the patients' committability. The legal rulings on the presumption of health are stringent. The courts "have repeatedly held that there should be a presumption of sanity. The burden of proof should be on the petitioners (i.e., the next of kin). There must be a preponderance of evidence and the evidence should be of a clear and unexceptional nature" (Scheff, 1964: 403). Given these rulings, it seems reasonable to argue, as I did in the article, that the committability of all patients except those rated at the extremes of dangerousness or impairment was uncertain. The ratings, I argued, suggested uncertainty about the committability of 63 percent of the patients in the sample—that is, those patients rated as neither dangerous nor severely impaired.

In the second phase of the study, when we observed the actual commitment procedures, we sought to find out how the psychiatric examiners and judges reacted to uncertainty. To summarize our observations, we found that *all* of the psychiatric examinations and judicial hearings that we witnessed were perfunctory. Furthermore, virtually every hearing resulted in a recommendation for commitment or continued hospitalization. The conclusion of the article is based not on the first phase only, but on both phases of the study. Since the first phase suggests uncertainty as to the committability of some of the patients, and since the second phase indicates that the commitment procedures were perfunctory in every instance of the sample—and yet resulted in continued hospitaliza-tion rather than release in virtually every case—the study appears to demonstrate the presumption of illness.

Gove's treatment of this article is somewhat irresponsible. By ignoring the second phase of the study, he takes the first phase out of context. Ignoring my argument concerning uncertainty, Gove suggests that had I placed the cutting point differently on the psychiatrists' ratings—that is, had I included as committable those patients rated as moderately impaired and/or somewhat likely to harm themselves—my data "would have shown instead that the vast majority of committed mental patients were mentally ill" (Gove, 1970b). He implies, therefore, that the results of my study rest entirely on my arbitrary choice of a cutting point.[2] In light of all the evidence presented in the article, where I placed the cutting point in the psychiatrists' ratings has little significance. Gove disregards the problem that the study posed: whether or not patients were being committed illegally. He misrepresents my conclusion by imputing to me the conclusion that most of the patients are not mentally ill. The study did not make this point, for I regard the criteria for mental illness as even more ambiguous than the legal standards for commitment.

Gove's other criticism of the study concerns the questionnaire given the psychiatrists to obtain ratings of dangerousness and mental impairment. He suggests that I should have provided the psychiatrists with descriptions of the behavior that the scales refer to. This criticism begs the question, however, for it seems to assume that there are precise psychiatric or legal criteria of committable behavior. In fact, the legal statutes, though they vary in language from state to state, are all vague, general, and ambiguous. They state simply that persons who are dangerous or unable to care for themselves may be committed if a strong case for commitment can be made. No statutes or psychiatric statements set forth behavioral criteria. My study sought not to help psychiatrists and judges interpret these vague laws, but to describe how they reacted to the law's ambiguity.

Some of Gove's criticism seems based on a misunderstanding of labeling theory. He seems to think that if the commitment rates reported in various studies are shown to be considerably less than 100 percent, this somehow refutes labeling theory (Gove, 1970a: 877–79). The argument made by labeling theorists that official agents of the societal reaction usually presume illness does not imply that commitment will always occur, any more than presuming innocence in criminal courts implies that acquittal will always occur. The primary question that labeling theory raises with respect to commitment rates is more complex than Gove implies. At what

---

[2] Gove's criticism of the cutting point applies more to an early report of some of the initial results of this study, a brief note in the *American Journal of Psychiatry* (Scheff, 1963). That report acknowledged that setting the cutting point on the psychiatrists' ratings was problematic (p. 268).

point and under what conditions does the process of denial stop and labeling begin? Gove apparently acknowledges that labeling occurs, but only in the last stages of the commitment funnel—that is, in the formal commitment procedure itself. I suspect that his formulation is much too simple, and that labeling occurs under some conditions much earlier in the process, even in the family or neighborhood; conversely, under some conditions denial may occur late in the process, as some of my studies showed (Scheff, 1966: 135).

The crucial question labeling theorists have raised vis-à-vis the medical model concerns contingencies leading to labeling that lie outside the patient and his behavior. For example, Greenley established that apart from a patient's psychiatric condition, the family's desire to bring him home seems to be the most powerful determinant of his length of hospitalization (Greenley, 1972). Labeling theory proposes that the patient's condition is only one of several contingencies affecting the societal reaction and, therefore, the patient's fate. Further contingencies are suggested in *Being Mentally Ill* (pp. 96–97). Gove's interpretation of labeling theory is simplistic and incorrect.

SUMMARIZING THE EVIDENCE

Inasmuch as most studies of "mental illness" were not designed to test labeling theory, seemingly plausible interpretations of most of them can be constructed either for or against labeling theory. Furthermore, since the conflict between labeling theory and the medical model engenders such furious partisanship, we should also exclude studies based on casual or unsystematic observations, in which the observer's bias is more likely to influence the results he reports. I have surveyed the research literature, therefore, for studies that meet two criteria. First, the studies must relate to labeling theory explicitly; second, their research methods must be systematic. At this writing, I have located eighteen studies that meet both criteria. Of these eighteen, only five—those by Gove (1973, 1974), Karmel (1969, 1970) and Robins (1966)—are inconsistent with labeling theory; the remainder—those by Denzin (1968), Denzin and Spitzer (1966), Greenley (1972), Haney and Michielutte (1968), Haney, Miller, and Michielutte (1969), Linsky (1970a, 1970b), Rosenhan (1973), Rushing (1971), Scheff (1964), Temerlin (1968), Wilde (1968), and Wenger and Fletcher (1969)—are consistent with labeling theory.

These eighteen studies vary widely in the reliability of the inferences that we can make from them. Five of the studies that are consistent with labeling theory use simple correlations—those by Denzin and Spitzer (1966); Denzin (1968); Haney and Michielutte (1968); and Haney, Miller, and Michielutte (1969). For example, Haney and his colleagues report positive correlations between commitment rates and the social characteristics of the patients and petitioners. He reports a higher rate of commitment for nonwhites than whites, for instance. Although his findings are consistent with labeling theory, they provide only very weak support for it because he has not controlled for the patient's condition. We are left with the question that occurs so often in social epidemiology: Are nonwhites committed more often because of the societal reaction to their social status, or because this particular social status is itself correlated with mental illness? That is, are nonwhites committed more often than whites because of their powerlessness, or because there is more mental illness among them? Haney's studies do not answer this question, nor do those by Denzin and Spitzer (1966), Denzin (1968), or Wenger and Fletcher (1969).

Similar criticism can be made of the two studies by Karmel (1969, 1970) that fail to support labeling theory. Based on interviews with patients after their hospitalization, her data fail to show any evidence of the acceptance of a deviant role as predicted by labeling theory. These are simple correlation studies with no controls (Bohr, 1970). Gove (1973) studied the amount and effects of stigma on a sample of ex-mental patients. His data indicate that the amount and effects of stigma were not very large, and the data therefore fail to support labeling theory. His data are somewhat ambiguous, however, because there is no control group of similar persons who were not hospitalized.

A series of much stronger studies, the findings of which support labeling theory, are those by Greenley (1972), Rushing (1971), Linsky (1970a), Scheff (1964), Wenger and Fletcher (1969) and Wilde (1968). I have already discussed my study. Greenley, whose 1972 study I cited above, studied the relationship between length of hospitalization and several social and psychiatric variables. He found that even when the patient's psychiatric condition is controlled, there is a strong relationship between the family desire for the patient's release and the length of hospitalization.

Rushing and Linsky each conducted studies of the relationship between psychiatric commitment and social class and other social characteristics. Because they indicated that their data overlap only partly, I cite both studies (Linsky, 1972; Rushing, 1972). Both experimenters used the same technique, which I believe controls for the patient's condition. If they had merely used commitment rates as their dependent variable, we would be left with this perplexing question: Are commitment rates higher in the lowest social class because there is more mental illness in that class, or for other reasons? (See the New Haven studies by Hollingshead and Redlich [1958].) However, both Rushing and Linsky used an index consisting of the ratio of involuntary to voluntary hospital admissions as a measure of societal reaction. I believe that such a ratio controls for gross variations in rates of mental illness. What the index provides, hopefully, is a measure of the most severe societal reaction—involuntary confinement—but with the phenomenon of mental illness at least partly controlled, assuming that voluntary commitments are equally "mentally ill." Perhaps this assumption should also be investigated. Both studies show a strong relationship between powerlessness and commitment rates. In the study by Wenger and Fletcher, the presence of a lawyer representing the patient in admission hearings decreased the likelihood of hospitalization. This relationship held within three degrees of manifest "mental illness."

The sixth of this group of studies, Wilde's (1968) study, concerns the relationship between the recommendations for commitment made by mental health examiners and various social characteristics of the pre-patients, with controls for the patient's psychiatric condition. In all five of these studies strong relationships are reported between commitment rates and such social characteristics as class, with psychiatric conditions controlled. These five studies support labeling theory because they indicate that the social characteristics of the patients help determine the severity of the societal reaction, independent of psychiatric condition.

The controlled studies by Robins (1966) and by Gove (1973) provide data that fail to support labeling theory. Robins used psychiatric diagnoses of adults who had been diagnosed when children as part of an evaluation of child-guidance clinics. Robins noted that some of the children that were diagnosed were treated and some were not. She argues that this data can be used to evaluate the effects of "the severity of societal response to the behavior problems of the children." She found that of the adults who received psychiatric treatment as children, 16 percent were diagnosed as having sociopathic personalities as adults; of the persons who did not receive psychiatric treatment as children, 24 percent were so diagnosed. Because the difference between the two percentages is not statistically significant, the hypothesis that psychiatric treatment was beneficial is not supported; but by the same token, neither is the labeling hypothesis that psychiatric treatment, particularly when involuntary, may stabilize behavior that would otherwise be transient. This finding is somewhat equivocal, however, because of the sampling problems of the original Cambridge-Somerville study.

Using a sample of hospitalized mental patients, Gove (1974) studied the relationship between the patient's psychiatric record and his economic and social resources. His data suggest that such resources facilitate treatment rather than allow the individual to avoid the societal reaction, and the data therefore support the medical model rather than labeling theory. Some caution is necessary in interpreting these findings, however, since patient characteristics were based on hospital data. For example, Gove finds that more of the records of patients with low resources present the patient as "never psychiatrically normal" than do the records of patients with higher resources. Does this mean that low-resource patients have been "mentally ill" longer, or that the hospital tends to construct their case histories in this way, retroactively (Goffman, 1959: 145)? In any case, Gove's interpretation of his data contradicts the conclusions of Linsky (1970a) and of Rushing (1971). Since the studies do not use the same indexes, it is not possible to compare them directly.

The final two studies to be discussed provide even stronger support for labeling theory than the other studies cited. The first, Temerlin's (1968), is a test of the influence of suggestion on psychiatric diagnosis. Temerlin finds that psychiatrists and clinical psychologists are extremely suggestible when they are diagnosing mental illness.

The study by Rosenhan (1973) took place in real settings—twelve mental hospitals. In this study, eight sane persons gained secret admittance to the different hospitals. In all twelve hospitals, the pseudopatients had enormous difficulty establishing that they were sane. The length of hospitalization ranged from seven to fifty-two days, with an average of nineteen days. The study's major finding is as follows:

Despite their public "show" of sanity, the pseudopatients were never detected. Admitted, except in one case, with a diagnosis of schizophrenia, each was discharged with a diagnosis of schizophrenia "in remission." The label "in remission" should in no way be dismissed as a formality, for at no time during any hospitalization had any question been raised about any pseudopatient's simulation. . . . the evidence is strong that once labeled schizophrenic, the pseudopatient was stuck with the label. (p. 252)

Rosenhan also collected a wide variety of subsidiary data dealing with the amount and quality of contact between the pseudopatients and the hospital staff. This data showed a strong tendency for the staff to treat the pseudopatients as nonpersons.

This study, like Temerlin's, strongly supports labeling theory. Both provide good models for future studies of labeling theory, the Rosenhan study with its use of actual hospital locations, and the Temerlin study with its experimental design.

We can now provisionally summarize the state of evidence concerning labeling theory. If we restrict ourselves to systematic studies related explicitly to labeling theory, eighteen are available. Of these, thirteen support labeling theory, and five fail to do so. Although the studies vary in reliability and precision, the balance of evidence seems to support labeling theory.

REFERENCES

BECKER, HOWARD.
    (1973)   "Labeling theory reconsidered." Pp. 177–208 in Outsiders. New York: Free Press.

BLUMER, HERBERT.
(1954)   "What is wrong with social theory?" American Journal of Sociology 19 (February): 3–10.

BOHR, RONALD H.
(1970)   Letter to the editor. Journal of Health and Social Behavior 11 (June): 52.

BRONOWSKI, J.
(1956)   Science and Human Values. New York: Harper & Row.
(1965)   The Identity of Man. Garden City, N.Y.: Doubleday, Natural History Press.

BRUYN, SEVERYN T.
(1966)   The Human Perspective in Sociology. Englewood Cliffs, N.J.: Prentice-Hall.

DAVIS, NANETTE J.
(1972)   "Labeling theory in deviance research: a critique and reconsideration." Sociological Quarterly 13 (Autumn): 447–74.

DENZIN, NORMAN K.
(1968)   "The self-fulfilling prophecy and patient-therapist interaction." Pp. 349–58 in Stephan P. Spitzer and Norman K. Denzin (eds.), The Mental Patient. New York: McGraw-Hill.

DENZIN, NORMAN K., AND STEPHAN P. SPITZER.
(1966)   "Paths to the mental hospital and staff predictions of patient role behavior." Journal of Health and Human Behavior 7 (Winter): 265–71.

GIBBS, JACK.
(1972)   "Issues in defining deviant behavior." Pp. 39–68 in Robert A. Scott and Jack D. Douglas (eds.), Theoretical Perspectives on Deviance. New York: Basic Books.

GOFFMAN, ERVING.
(1959)   Asylums. Garden City, N.Y.: Doubleday Anchor.

GOVE, WALTER.
(1970a)   "Societal reaction as an explanation of mental illness: an evaluation." American Sociological Review 35 (October): 873–84.
(1970b)   "Who is hospitalized: a critical review of some sociological studies of mental illness." Journal of Health and Human Behavior 11 (December): 294–304.
(1973)   "The stigma of mental hospitalization." Archives of General Psychiatry 28 (April): 494–500.
(1974)   "Individual resources and mental hospitalization: a comparison and evaluation of the societal reaction and psychiatric perspectives." American Sociological Review (February): 86–100.

GREENLEY, JAMES R.
(1972)   "The psychiatric patient's family and length of hospitalization." Journal of Health and Social Behavior 13 (March): 25–37.

HANEY, C. ALLEN, AND ROBERT MICHIELUTTE.
(1968)   "Selective factors operating in the adjudication of incompetency." Journal of Health and Social Behavior 9 (September): 233–242.

HANEY, C. ALLEN, KENT S. MILLER, AND ROBERT MICHIELUTTE.
(1969) "The interaction of petitioner and deviant social characteristics in the adjudication of incompetency." Sociometry 32 (June): 182–93.

HOLLINGSHEAD, AUGUST B., AND FREDERICH C. REDLICH.
(1958) Social Class and Mental Illness. New York: John Wiley.

KARMEL, MADELINE.
(1969) "Total institution and self-mortification." Journal of Health and Social Behavior 10 (June): 134–41.

(1970) "The internalization of social roles in institutionalized chronic mental patients." Journal of Health and Social Behavior 11 (September): 231–35.

LAING, RONALD, AND AARON ESTERSON.
(1964) Sanity, Madness, and the Family. London: Tavistock.

LINSKY, ARNOLD S.
(1970a) "Community homogeneity and exclusion of the mentally ill: reaction and consensus about deviance." Journal of Health and Social Behavior 11 (December): 304–11.

(1970b) "Who shall be excluded: the influence of personal attributes in community reaction to the mentally ill." Social Psychiatry 5 (July): 166–71.

(1972) Letter. American Journal of Sociology 78 (November): 684–86.

ROBINS, LEE.
(1966) Deviant Children Grown Up. Baltimore: Williams & Wilkins.

ROSENHAN, DAVID L.
(1973) "On being sane in insane places." Science 179 (January): 250–58.

RUSHING, WILLIAM A.
(1971) "Individual resources, societal reaction, and hospital commitment." American Journal of Sociology 77 (November): 511–26.

(1972) Letter. American Journal of Sociology 78 (November): 686–88.

SCHEFF, THOMAS J.
(1963) "Legitimate, transitional, and illegitimate mental patients in a midwestern state." American Journal of Psychiatry 120 (September): 267–69.

(1964) "The societal reaction to deviance: ascriptive elements in the psychiatric screening of mental patients in a midwestern state." Social Problems 11 (Spring): 401–13.

(1966) Being Mentally Ill: A Sociological Theory. Chicago: Aldine.

SCHUTZ, ALFRED.
(1962) The Problem of Social Reality: Collected Papers I. The Hague: Martinus Nijhoff.

SCHWARTZ, J., AND G. L. BAUM.
(1957) "The history of histoplasmosis." New England Journal of Medicine 256 (February): 253–58.

TEMERLIN, MAURICE K.
(1968) "Suggestion effects in psychiatric diagnosis." Journal of Nervous and Mental Disease 147 (4): 349–53.

WENGER, DENNIS L., AND C. RICHARD FLETCHER.
(1969) "The effect of legal counsel on admissions to a state mental hospital: a confrontation of professions." Journal of Health and Social Behavior 10 (June): 66–72.
WILDE, WILLIAM A.
(1968) "Decision-making in a psychiatric screening agency." Journal of Health and Social Behavior 9 (September): 215–21.
YARROW, MARIAN RADKE, CHARLOTTE GREEN SCHWARTZ, HARRIET S. MURPHY, AND LEILA CALHOUN DEASY.
(1955) "The psychological meaning of mental illness in the family." Journal of Social Issues 11 (4): 12–24.

4

ALTERNATIVE VIEWS OF THE PSYCHIATRIST'S ROLE

James R. Greenley

Chapters 4–6 represent some of the stronger (and more readable) studies that provide support for the labeling theory of mental illness. Goffman has argued in his book Asylums *that the medical model, which focuses only on the "patient," obscures reality:*

> *The society's official view is that inmates of mental hospitals are there primarily because they are suffering from mental illness. However, in the degree that the "mentally ill" outside hospitals numerically approach or surpass those inside hospitals, one could say that mental patients distinctively suffer not from mental illness, but from contingencies. (p. 135)*

One such contingency is the patient's family, and how they feel about having the patient with them. Greenley's study supports the labeling theory contention that this social fact, the family's willingness to keep the patient, is as important as the patient's medical or legal status in determining his fate.

Reprinted from *Social Problems*, Vol. 20, No. 2, Fall 1972.
The author wishes to acknowledge the help and advice received from Jerome K. Myers and A. B. Hollingshead during the course of this research. David Mechanic made many helpful comments on earlier drafts of this paper. Calculation of significance levels for partial Gammas was made possible through the advice of Donald Ploch.

This paper reports research concerning alternative views of the role of the psychiatrist in the inpatient setting. First, the psychiatrist, as a service professional, is seen as an expert supplying advice and direction to patients who come seeking it (Goffman, 1961: 324ff). The psychiatrist observes, diagnoses, prescribes, and treats in the medical tradition. What the patient does or has done to him follows from the psychiatrist's expert assessment and direction. When action taken toward the patient, such as a discharge, does not appear to be the result of the professional's advice or evaluation, such action is often attributed to the interference of outside influences such as the state (Szasz, 1968; Leifer, 1969) or the patient's family (Hollingshead and Redlich, 1958:343; Myers and Roberts, 1959:217). Second, Goffman (1961:380) and others (Szasz, 1968; Simmons et al., 1956) imply that decisions concerning the psychiatric inpatient are not made so much by an expert, the psychiatric professional, as through a complex process of negotiation among interested and influential parties. The patient, his family, the hospital nursing staff, the hospital administration, community agencies, and the police, as well as the psychiatrist, are among those variously noted as involved and influential in decisions made about the patient. In this view, the psychiatrist is seen as functioning in large part to ✓ supply medical-psychiatric explanations or rationales for decisions often made on other grounds by other people (Goffman, 1961:384). The psychiatrist is viewed as legitimizing actions taken toward the patient by supplying the traditional medical-psychiatric reasons for it. These two views of the psychiatrist's role imply very different relationships between the psychiatrist's expert evaluations and the patient's treatment experiences.

Data from a study of decisions on the timing of patient discharges from an inpatient unit are used here to suggest an answer to the question of which view of the psychiatrist's role best typifies what psychiatrists actually do in inpatient services. The data were gathered primarily to assess the impact of the wishes of families and patients on length of hospitalization (Greenley, 1970). These data show that the desires of patients and their families strongly influence the timing of release. I shall examine the two views of the psychiatrist's role by exploring the ways these desires affect the timing of release.

SETTING AND METHOD

One six-ward "unit" of a large state mental institution in New England, serving a specified geographical area, was the site of this research. Extensive informal observations were made of day-to-day contacts between patients and their psychiatrists.[1] From thirty to several hundred

---

[1] The unit's psychiatric staff includes consulting psychiatrists, from both the community and a local prestigious Eastern university, who supervise residents and handle intake and

hours were spent in each of a variety of settings: nursing stations, patient-patient interaction at meals and on the ward, records room, nursing supervisor's office, staff dining room, staff coffee lounge, truck landing where patients congregated, central lobby of hospital building, and staff conferences concerning patients. Private, semistructured interviews were conducted with most administrative personnel on this unit, several social workers, and most of the psychiatrists.

In addition, 342 structured interviews were conducted with the patients, families, and psychiatrists involved in 125 consecutive admissions to this unit between May and September, 1969. All patients in the sample were 21 to 65 years old. None of the sample patients was diagnosed as suffering primarily from drug addiction, alcoholism, or senility, since other units at this hospital were designated to treat these patients. Initial interviews were obtained separately with the psychiatrist and the patient, with few exceptions, during the first week of the patient's hospitalization. Reinterviews with the patient and his psychiatrist occurred after three weeks of the patient's hospitalization. At this latter time (before the patient's release), members of the patient's family were interviewed in their homes.

Thirty-nine percent of attempted initial interviews with the psychiatrists were not obtained because the psychiatrists refused to participate, regardless of whom their patients were. Because patients were assigned to psychiatrists by intake personnel on a rotational basis, there is no reason to suspect a systematic bias to result from the loss of these cases. A second interview was sought from all patients and psychiatrists from whom initial interviews were obtained. Refusal rates for the second interviews with psychiatrists, for both the interviews with patients and for the family interviews, ranged from 0 percent to 11 percent. Chi-square goodness of fit tests showed no significant difference between the completed cases for each schedule and the 125 originally selected admission cases, on the following patient characteristics: sex, age, marital status, religion, occupation, education, social class, and previous admission to a psychiatric hospital.[2]

Professional judgments of patient's psychiatric impairment were gathered by asking each psychiatrist, "How psychiatrically impaired is this

---

disposition staffings; resident psychiatrists, most of whom are foreign born and trained; and nonpsychiatrically-trained M.D.'s who are administrators and have years of experience working with psychiatric patients.

[2] The categories of the control variables used here and throughout this study are as follows: Age—21–30, 31–40, 41–50, 51–65; Race—white, Negro (three of the 125 cases were eliminated from this analysis because they were Puerto Rican); Religion—Protestant, Catholic (11 of the 125 cases were dropped from this analysis because they listed themselves as "none," "Jewish," or "other"); Marital status—married, single, divorced or widowed or separated; Education—less than 7 years, 7–9 years, 10–12 years, some college, completed college, graduate work done; Occupation—seven categories used as given in A. B. Hollingshead's Two Factor Index of Social Position, Social Class—five categories used as computed by A. B. Hollingshead's Two Factor Index of Social Position.

patient now?" and giving him six discrete response categories ranging from "very severely impaired" to "no visible impairment." Using similar direct questions and discrete response categories, each psychiatrist was asked how psychiatrically impaired the patient was relative to other patients, and how much the patient needed to be in the hospital.

Desires concerning release held by the patient and a family member were measured by asking each separately whether they wished release or retention. Ninety-two percent of the patients and 94 percent of the family members gave a clear and unambiguous reply to this question. Using these patient and family replies, a combined index of family and patient desires was constructed. The four logically possible ways these family and patient desires could be aligned were ordered, beginning with the one most often associated with a patient's longest stay and continuing to the one where the patient's likelihood of remaining was the least. The resulting alignments, ordered as in Figure 1, form a combined index of family and patient desires on which each case is located.

FIGURE 1.

COMBINED FAMILY AND PATIENT DESIRES INDEX

Possible alignments between family & patient	Family	Patient
A	+	+
B	+	−
C	−	+
D	−	−

" + " *indicates the party wants the patient to remain hospitalized.*
" − " *indicates the party wants the patient to leave the hospital.*

The outcome of the release decision was measured by length of hospitalization. Patients left the hospital during one of five relatively distinct periods: 1–4 days, 5–20 days, 21–36 days, 37–100 days, and over 100 days from admission. Only by treating the variable length of hospitalization in terms of these five ordered categories can the realities of this hospital's organization and the attitudes of its staff be taken into account.

RESULTS

In this study, as was found by Watt and Buglass (1966), when psychiatrists thought patients were more impaired, the patients remained hospitalized longer (see Table 1, column 1). Psychiatrist's estimates of both patient's absolute and relative psychiatric impairment are substantially and significantly related to length of hospitalization within all categories of the eight basic control variables used in this study.

TABLE 1
LENGTH OF HOSPITALIZATION AND PSYCHIATRIC IMPAIRMENT

Measure of Psychiatric Impairment	No control variable	Control Variables		
		Combined Desires of Family and Patient	Desires of Patient's Family	Desires of the Patient
	N = 63	N = 34	N = 42	N = 58
General Psychiatric Impairment				
Gamma or Partial Gamma	.44	.02	.14	.17
Level of Significance	**	NS	NS	NS
Relative Psychiatric Impairment				
Gamma or Partial Gamma	.55	.02	.25	.49
Level of Significance	***	NS	NS	*

*** indicates p < .001; ** indicates p < .01; * indicates p < .05; and NS indicates p > .05.

Furthermore, psychiatric impairment is strongly and positively related to the psychiatrist's judgment of the patient's need for further hospitalization.[3] Responses to the psychiatric impairment questions are thus used as indicators of the psychiatrist's general view of the patient's psychiatric problems.

The combined family- and patient-desires index is also strongly and positively associated with length of hospitalization, as shown in Table 2, column 1. The desires of the patient's family member regarding discharge are themselves even more strongly and positively associated with the actual length of the patient's hospitalization (see Table 2, column 1). The more the patient's family member expressed a desire for the patient to remain hospitalized, the longer the patient did in fact remain. Similarly, the desires of the patient concerning discharge are positively associated with the length of his hospitalization. The more the patient desired release, the shorter the hospitalization.

The combined family-and-patient-desires index is strongly related to the psychiatrist's impairment estimates. When the patient and family both desired release, the patient was rated as less impaired.[4]

[3] The general measure of psychiatric impairment and the estimate of need for hospitalization associated positively with Gamma = .61, p < .001, N = 62. The relative measure of psychiatric impairment associated positively with estimates of need for hospitalization, with Gamma = .66, p < .001, N = 63.

[4] This index relates to the general psychiatric impairment estimate, with Gamma = .54, p < .001, N = 34; it relates to the relative measure of psychiatric impairment, with Gamma = .51, p < .001, N = 34.

TABLE 2
LENGTH OF HOSPITALIZATION AND FAMILY
AND PATIENT DESIRES

Measure of Family or Patient Desires	Length of Hospitalization		
	No control variable	Control Variables	
		General Psychiatric Impairment	Relative Psychiatric Impairment
Combined desires of family and patient			
Gamma or Partial Gamma	.52	.50	.60
Level of Significance	***	**	***
N	(64)	(34)	(34)
Desires of the Patient's Family			
Gamma or Partial Gamma	.78	.74	.83
Level of Significance	***	***	***
N	(80)	(42)	(42)
Desires of the Patient			
Gamma or Partial Gamma	.35	.27	.47
Level of Significance	***	NS	*
N	(113)	(58)	(58)

*** indicates p < .001; ** indicates p < .01; * indicates p < .05; NS indicates p > .05.

The relationships between length of hospitalization and the psychiatric impairment measures are greatly reduced in most cases when the desires of the patient and family are statistically controlled (see Table 1). Only in one instance is the reduction not substantial—that is, controlling for desires of the patient alone—and then only for one of the two measures of psychiatric impairment. A variable such as patient desires, which is less strongly related to length of hospitalization, might be expected to have less of an effect on the relationship between length of hospitalization and other variables. The fact that patient desires have less effect on length of hospitalization than do family desires is discussed in more detail elsewhere (Greenley, 1972). Central to the present analysis is the combined effect of family and patient desires.

The relationships between length of hospitalization and measures of family and patient desires are in general not reduced when the psychiatrist's estimate of psychiatric impairment is statistically controlled (see Table 2). The wishes of the family, and to a lesser extent the patient, appear to have an impact on length of hospitalization apart from the psychiatrist's estimate of the patient's psychiatric condition.

These results suggest that some possible ways these variables might be causally related are clearly more probable than others. In particular, three possible causal explanations appear unlikely. First, the psychiatrists' impairment estimates probably do not influence length of hospitalization independently of the desires of the patient and family. Otherwise, the relationship between psychiatrists' impairment estimates and length of hospitalization would not be reduced when family and patient desires are statistically controlled. Second, psychiatrists' impairment estimates probably do not bring about both family desires and lengths of hospitalization independently. If this were the case, the relationship between psychiatrists' impairment estimates and length of hospitalization would not be reduced when the desires of the family and patient are statistically controlled. Also, in this case, the relationship of family and patient desires to length of hospitalization would be reduced when psychiatrists' impairment estimates are controlled. Third, it is not likely that family and patient desires influence the psychiatrists' impairment estimates and these in turn affect length of hospitalization. If this causal sequence were correct, the relationshp between psychiatrists' impairment estimates and length of hospitalization would not be reduced when the desires of family and patient are statistically controlled. Also, the relationship between family and patient desires and length of hospitalization would have been reduced when psychiatrists' impairment estimates are controlled. None of these three possible causal relationships is supported by the data.

There are two other causal sequences that are congruent with the above data. First, psychiatrists' impairment estimates may influence family and patient desires and these in turn might affect length of hospitalization. Second, desires of the family and patient might independently influence both length of hospitalization and the psychiatrists' impairment estimates. These two explanations differ in that the first suggests that families and patients are influenced by psychiatrists' impairment estimates and the second suggests that psychiatrists' impairment estimates follow from family and patient desires. To distinguish between these two possibilities, we will focus largely on other data concerning the patient's family, since family desires clearly are more important determinants of length of hospitalization.

The families' desires remain virtually unchanged during the three-week period studied (in only 14 percent of the cases did change occur, $N = 61$), even though the ratings of psychiatric impairment changed in 63 percent of the 30 cases on which there is full comparable family data. In no case do family desires change over time to conform better with what would be expected on the basis of the impairment ratings. Families do not appear to base their desires for further hospitalization on what they may be told by the psychiatrist about the patient's psychiatric impairment.

The psychiatrists' impairment estimates changed in the majority of cases. A few patients were psychiatrically reevaluated at the end of three weeks in a manner more congruent with the desires of the family; there were about the same number of cases in which psychiatrists' reevaluations were less congruent with family desires. When only major shifts in the psychiatrist's impairment estimate are inspected (changes unlikely to be due to measurement error), 6 of 9 cases are shifts by the psychiatrist that make his impairment estimate more congruent with the wishes of the patient's family.[5] Though these data do not strongly confirm or deny that psychiatrist's impairment estimates may be caused in part by family desires, it does make this proposition worth consideration.

Some families might change their views within the first few days of the patient's hospitalization, and thus evidence no change during the three-week period studied. Forty-nine percent of the families reported having contact with the psychiatrist (by phone, letter, or in person) by the time the psychiatrist was first interviewed. Thus, half of the families could have learned directly of the psychiatrist's impairment estimate during these first few days. Though it is also possible that families learned early from patients about psychiatrists' evaluations, it is improbable that patients could have transmitted much of this information from the psychiatrist to the family. Only 21 percent of the patients had a correct view of the psychiatrists' feelings about whether they needed to be hospitalized, and only a third of these had any contact at all with the family by the time of the first patient interview. Thus, less than 10 percent of the patient's could have carried the psychiatrist's view to the family. A slightly larger percentage (24 percent) of the patients knew correctly what the family desires were by the time of the first interview. Either through these patients or directly from the family, psychiatrists might have learned what the family wanted. By the time of the first interview, 60 percent of the psychiatrists knew correctly what the family wanted. Therefore, we conclude that it is no more likely that families had changed their views to conform to the psychiatrists by the time of the first interview than vice versa.

DISCUSSION

In the informal interviews, most of the psychiatrists confirmed what the structured-interview data appear to show: patients' families had the ability to effect a discharge or prevent a release. As one therapist put it, "It's hard to stand up to a family, which is quite funny since we are

---

[5] Psychiatrists rated impairment in one of six ordered categories: very severely impaired, severely impaired, moderately impaired, mildly impaired, very slightly impaired, no visible impairment. A major shift in the psychiatrist's estimate is defined as a shift from one category to a nonadjacent category.

supposed to be a professional group." Only a small minority of the psychiatrists interviewed denied consistently that families were sometimes more influential in release decisions than they themselves were.

The structured-interview data do not indicate clearly that psychiatrists are influencing family and patient desires or that psychiatrists' impairment estimates are being influenced by them. It is possible and probable that both of these processes are occurring simultaneously. Yet, considerable information gathered in informal observations and interviews leads me to favor the argument that family and patient desires do influence psychiatrists' estimates.

In general, the psychiatrists expressed little anger, resentment, or disappointment when such family or patient pressures threatened to or did take precedence over their discharge decisions. In many decision areas a large number of presumed and acknowledged intrusions into the psychiatrist's professional realm were observed, such as aides requesting medication changes to make patient control easier, administrators seeking changes in patient care for administrative reasons, and courts demanding release or retention unexpectedly. Yet almost no complaints about these intrusions were lodged formally, and exceedingly few were even expressed informally (such as among therapists over coffee) or in response to direct questions by the researcher. For example, in the area of release decisions, among those few patients evaluated as severely ill but who nevertheless left the hospital relatively early, there were no discharges "against medical advice." Similarly, most families who pressured successfully to remove a patient from the hospital against the wishes of the psychiatrist did not have to secure releases "against medical advice." In general, there were very few overt indications that psychiatrists felt that outside influences, even effective ones, were unjust intrusions on their practice of psychiatry.

Psychiatrists rarely complained openly about family or patient influences, thereby acknowledging their impact on the discharge process; rather, psychiatrists routinely explained discharge decisions by reference to their professional psychiatric evaluations and treatments. The patient's impairment or improvement was the reason commonly given for release or retention; for example, psychiatrists would tell patients that they were too sick to leave. The psychiatrists almost always explained their actions to each other, to the researchers, and in the records, in terms of the traditional observation-diagnoses-prescription-treatment scheme.

Such medical-psychiatric reasons could continue to be given in the face of admittedly efficacious family and patient pressure if the expert psychiatric evaluations were themselves influenced by family and patient pressures. Estimates of impairment were at times seen to follow from an expected or actual outcome of the discharge process—for instance, the physical presence or absence of the patient at the hospital. Therapists made comments such as "If she was the least bit sick, she would never have left the hospital," or to a patient, "You would not be here if you weren't sick!" In this way, being in or out of the hospital appeared to produce perceptions of persons as sick, well, recovered, and so forth (cf. Goffman, 1961). In addition, the psychiatrist's view of the person's impairment seemed at times to grow to reflect the likely outcome. If the patient was expected to exit soon, he sometimes came to be seen as less impaired. If the patient and family were eager for release, in the vast majority of instances this was interpreted as a sign of "health." Patient desires for release were most often seen as negative characteristics when chances for discharge were slim—for example, when the family refused to take the patient home (the patient was being unrealistic and was resisting treatment). Even more common, in this vein, when a patient wanted to stay, others developed perceptions of him as "sick." Thus, when one psychiatrist noted a patient's desire for further hospitalization, he said, "Well, it's not all that good. They may like it here, but you have to be pretty sick to like it here." Or, as another staff person put it, "If anyone wants to stay here, believe me, they are crazy." However legitimate these family and patient desires are as indicators to the psychiatrist of the patient's pathology or health, their use demonstrates the impact of family and patient desires on psychiatric evaluations.

In addition, psychiatrists were occasionally observed altering their views of patients' psychiatric conditions over time in response to new family or patient pressures. When one social worker reported that a family would not accept a patient whom his therapist wished to discharge to them, the therapist concluded, "He needs hospitalization and has no place to go," and recommended transfer to a nearby Veterans Hospital for "long-term care." And as another psychiatrist explained concerning diagnostic evaluations, "Sometimes when a family calls and says they don't want to see someone again, I know that my [neurotic] diagnosis is wrong and that they are probably schizophrenic. If the family doesn't want them, they are usually more sick than I think, so I change and call them schizophrenic." Numerous such instances were observed in which the influence of patient or family may have become translated into congruent estimates of the patient's pathology.

It is possible that even when discharge recommendations do follow from family and patient pressures, medical-psychiatric explanations for discharge decisions should be expected. These explanations might serve to confirm, legitimate, and in other ways make congruent perceived reality with actual or anticipated reality. Thus, even when a psychiatrist says, "You are well enough to go now," he remains consistent with the view that his job functions to supply medical-psychiatric reasons for decisions made on other grounds.

CONCLUSION

The interview and observational data suggest that to some degree family and patient desires influence psychiatrists' impairment estimates. The data also suggest that psychiatrists may indirectly affect the timing of release through their influence on patient and family wishes. With no desire to minimize the importance and implications of this latter possibility, we will conclude by exploring the nature and basis of a psychiatrist's role where psychiatrists' evaluations of pathology do not determine treatment decision as much as they reflect the desires of the patient and his family.

When confronted with nonmedical forces that are pressuring him, the psychiatrist may resist, and if effective, may prevail. Yet in doing so, he may also put his authority on the line. His authority, as all authority, is given him by his followers. If he too consistently takes stands inconsistent with his client's desires, he may find his once-faithful fleeing elsewhere. Thus, he may from time to time find reasons to "prescribe" that which his followers, the family and patient in this case, desire. As a service professional, his ability to lead others depends partially on how convinced they are of the wisdom of his advice.

The psychiatrist may be more likely to curry the favor of his clients than other professionals are. Most professionals, the psychiatrist included, are granted the respect and the following of their clients on the basis of past proved worth. The client returns to the TV repairman or the surgeon because this professional has successfully rectified his problem in the past. Upon bringing his television home from the TV repair shop, the client may feel confident that it functions because the repairman worked on it. After a therapy session, he may be less sure that his psychiatrist has done him any good. The criteria for judging the technical competence of psychiatrists are known to be relatively slim. The psychiatrist may be more repsonsive to his clients' pressures because he may be more vulnerable to their fickle judgments of his services. In general, there may be a greater tendency for practitioners to bow to the wishes of their clients in those professions where there exists some difficulty in judging the technical competence of the professional's work.

One might expect that to the extent that such a pattern is characteristic of psychiatric practice, it would be less pronounced or even nonexistent in those areas of psychiatric inpatient practice where there is more concrete evidence of specific goals being met (behavior therapy?) or where therapy is, or is supposed to be, of greater quality (university or other prestigious centers of care?). Similarly, as disciplines, including psychiatry, grow in demonstrable technical competence, they would presumably have to rely less and less on such responsiveness to nonprofessional pressures.

A psychiatrist functioning to legitimize decisions made on other grounds may accomplish some of the same goals as he would functioning in a traditionally conceived medical-psychiatric role. He can act so as to avoid unwanted conflict, tensions, and feelings between parties he is serving— such as the patient, his relatives, and the institution. For instance, when the patient's family refuses to take the patient home, the psychiatrist can tell him he is "too sick to leave," and in doing so he consoles the patient, who feels mistreated, and earns the respect and gratitude of the family for alleviating their guilt (they, of course, are not the ones who said he was too sick). If the hospital administration, having decided it no longer wishes to care for a patient, arranges a transfer of the patient to an "undesirable" institution, the psychiatrist can "prescribe" the transfer, removing the institutional hierarchy from the glare of responsibility and helping the family accept the move as in the best interests of their loved one. To the extent that treatments are recommended for such reasons, the psychiatrist may be largely prescribing remedies for interpersonal and organizational conflicts. Many therapists, in fact, would consider dealing with such problems as part of their job.

In addition, the psychiatrist may have a definite impact on the outcome even while performing basically a legitimizing function. He might cure the patient, for instance, thereby directly influencing pressures from the family and patient. If such crucial factors are altered, a family may be willing to take a patient home, or a ward staff might be less likely to push for a patient's discharge. Yet although such therapeutic intervention may attest to the psychiatrist's expertise, it does not indicate that his role relationship with the patient is necessarily one of expert professional to client.

In order to perform legitimizing functions, the psychiatrist would have to have the flexibility to prescribe almost any treatment for any patient. Without such capability, the therapist could be caught having no grounds on which to prescribe that which must be done for other reasons. The Freudian analytic scheme appears ideally suited to this task and may, we can speculate, derive some of its popularity from this property. Further-more, the skills required for this task, not being legitimate for texts in psychiatry, would have to be acquired informally. In fact, psychiatrists may learn such things "clinically" without ever being taught at all.

These observations can, of course, be valid and useful only to the extent that psychiatrists do indeed make expert pronouncements to help fulfill the desires of influential individuals. Caution must be exercised in generalizing from the results of this study. The data presented derive from a small, although carefully studied, sample from one hospital setting only, and from examination of only one type of decision, the discharge decision. Further work might involve multiple inpatient services and several kinds of decisions. This study suggests only that evidence can be gathered in support or refutation of these views of the psychiatrist's role.

REFERENCES

GOFFMAN, E.
(1961) Asylums. New York: Anchor Books.
GREENLEY, J. R.
(1970) "Exit from a mental hospital." Unpublished Ph.D. dissertation, Yale University.
(1972) "The psychiatric patient's family and length of hospitalization." Journal of Health and Social Behavior 13 (March): 25-37.
HOLLINGSHEAD, A. B., AND F. C. REDLICH.
(1958) Social Class and Mental Illness. New York: John Wiley.
LEIFER, R.
(1969) In the Name of Mental Health. New York: Science House.
MYERS, J. K., AND B. H. ROBERTS.
(1959) Family and Class Dynamics in Mental Illness. New York: John Wiley.
SIMMONS, O. G., J. A. DAVIS, AND K. SPENCER.
(1956) "Interpersonal strains in release from a mental hospital." Social Problems 4 (July): 21-28.
SZASZ, T. S.
(1968) Law, Liberty, and Psychiatry. New York: Macmillan, Collier Books.
WATT, D., AND D. BUGLASS.
(1966) "The effect of clinical and social factors on the discharge of chronic psychiatric patients." Social Psychiatry 1 (October): 57-63.

5

SUGGESTION EFFECTS IN PSYCHIATRIC DIAGNOSIS

Maurice K. Temerlin

Several studies have suggested that once the process of civil commitment of the "mentally ill" has begun, there is usually a "presumption of illness." Once a person has been labeled mentally ill, there is a strong tendency for officials to see him as indeed mentally ill, regardless of his actual condition. This tendency is predicted by labeling theory, and is directly contrary to both the medical model and legal proscriptions. The following study provides strong support for the labeling-theory position.

In order to explore interpersonal influences that might affect psychiatric diagnosis, psychiatrists, clinical psychologists, and graduate students in clinical psychology diagnosed a sound-recorded interview with a normal, healthy man. Just before listening to the interview, they heard a professional person of high prestige, acting as a confederate of the experimenter, say that the individual to be diagnosed was "a very interesting man because he looked neurotic but actually was quite psychotic."

CRITERIA OF MENTAL HEALTH

Since people are not perfect and any imperfection could be considered evidence of mental illness, a professional actor was trained to portray a mentally healthy man by these criteria: he was happy and effective in his work; he established a warm, gracious, and satisfying relationship with the interviewer; he was self-confident and secure, but without being arrogant, competitive, or grandiose. He was identified with the parent of the same sex, was happily married and in love with his wife, and consistently enjoyed sexual intercourse. He felt that sex was fun, unrelated to anxiety, social-role conflict, or status striving. This was built into his role because mental patients allegedly are sexually anhedonic. He was also defined as an empirically oriented agnostic, because mental patients so often are committed to religion, mysticism, extrasensory perception, or occult phenomenon; he also had a benign, self-reflexive sense of humor to counteract the common impression that mental patients are humorless people who lack insight. He had no hallucinations, delusions, or psychosomatic symptoms, and he also was provided with a happy childhood.

Since even the healthiest people presumably have anxieties related to difficult life situations, the actor expressed mild concern over Vietnam, had occasional disagreements with his wife over whether to go to church or stay in bed on Sunday morning, and did not always know precisely how best to raise his children. To give him a reason for being in a clinical setting which would not automatically classify him as sick, the script defined him as a successful and productive physical scientist and

This study was supported in part by the faculty research fund of the University of Oklahoma. Mr. William Trousdale helped gather the data for this study, and Jane Chapman, William Lemmon, Ruth Mansfield, and Robert Ragland read the manuscript and made many helpful suggestions. From *Journal of Nervous and Mental Disease*, 147: 349–358, 1968.

mathematician (a profession as far away from psychiatry as possible) who had read a book on psychotherapy and wanted to talk about it.

PROCEDURE

The actor memorized a script in which he described himself and his life. The context of the script and the relaxed way in which he portrayed it met the above criteria, as judged by three clinical psychologists (evaluating the interview without prior suggestion) and the control groups to be described later. He then was interviewed by the author as if he were a prospective patient. The actor knew the interview was being sound-recorded, but he did not know the purpose of the experiment or that the recording would be diagnosed by 45 graduate students in clinical psychology, 25 practicing clinical psychologists, and 25 psychiatrists. (A transcription of the interview is available upon request.) Psychologists and psychiatrists were selected from three cities on a stratified random basis to represent employment in clinics, state mental hospitals, Veterans hospitals, and private practice. Graduate students were enrolled in APA-approved doctoral programs in clinical psychology at two Midwestern state universities.

The sound-recorded interview was played for the staff, interns, residents, and consultants of the participating hospitals and clinics, ostensibly as part of a regular staff meeting, practicum meeting, research seminar, or in-service training program in diagnostic interviewing. Shortly before the tape was played, the prestige confederate remarked that the patient on the tape was "a very interesting man because he looks neurotic, but actually is quite psychotic." To the clinical psychologists and graduate students, the confederate was a well-known psychologist with many professional honors. Psychiatrists were told that "two board-certified psychiatrists, one also a psychoanalyst, had found the recording interesting because the patient looked neurotic but actually was quite psychotic. However, two diagnostic opinions are not enough for a criterial diagnosis against which test scores can be correlated in a test construction project."

After listening to the interview, the subjects indicated their diagnosis on a data sheet that listed, in counterbalanced order, 10 psychoses, 10 neuroses, and 10 miscellaneous personality types, one of which was "normal or healthy personality." After circling the category that best fit the patient, the subjects were asked to:

Write a brief description of the patient to indicate the behavioral basis of your diagnosis. Be as descriptive as you can. Use no technical terms, and make as few inferences as possible. Just write what you heard the patient say that led you to diagnose him as you did.

After they wrote the clinical report, the subjects were asked to change their original diagnosis if they wished, the prediction being that initial diagnoses would be corrected after observations and inferences were separated in the task of writing the clinical report.

Acting as confederates, other "subjects" conducted an informal "grapevine" debriefing to see if compliance with the suggestion had been conscious, to check on subject naïveté (harder to control as the experiment progressed), and to see if the subjects had been suspicious of the procedure. After all data were collected, formal debriefings were conducted; those subjects whose diagnoses were correct were interviewed at length.

CONTROLS

Four control groups were used. Three matched groups, stratified for professional identity, diagnosed the same recorded interview under different conditions. One diagnosed it with no prior suggestion; another diagnosed it with the prestige suggestion reversed. To control that a clinical setting alone might predispose a diagnostician to expect pathology, one group evaluated the interview as part of a project for selecting scientists to work in industrial research. These subjects were asked to listen to a sound recording of a "new kind of personnel interview, designed to obtain personal information related to scientific productivity," and then to evaluate a candidate for employment on ten employment-relevant scales, such as responsibility, probable scientific productivity, and relationships with colleagues and supervisors. Embedded among these distracter scales was a mental-health scale with health and psychosis at the extremes and neurosis in the center. The first thirty seconds of the recording were changed to delete curiosity about psychotherapy and to substitute a personnel manager for a clinician; otherwise, the interview remained unchanged.

As a fourth control, a mock sanity hearing was conducted in a county courthouse with lay jurors randomly selected from a regular jury wheel.[1] Jurors judged the same interview after being told that the court was experimenting with a new procedure for conducting sanity hearings, with the jury listening to a recording of the diagnostic interview itself rather than relying exclusively on psychiatric testimony.

RESULTS

Control data are presented in Table 1. The diagnoses of experimental subjects are presented in Table 2. All differences between experimental

[1] For this control group, I am grateful to Dr. Helen Klein, who conducted the mock sanity hearing.

TABLE 1

DIAGNOSES OF CONTROL SUBJECTS

	Mental Illness		
	Psychosis	Neurosis and character disorder	Mental Health
No prestige suggestion (N = 21*)	0	9	12
Suggestion of mental health (N = 20*)	0	0	20
Employment interview (N = 24*)	0	7	17
Sanity hearing† (N = 12)	0	−‡	12

* Totals after a replication, grouped together when no differences were found on replication.
† Jurors voted individually, then after discussion, with the same results.
‡ In the sanity hearing, jurors voted "sane" or "insane" to follow legal procedures as closely as possible.

and control groups are significant at the .01 level, whether comparisons are made between specific groups or combined groups. For example, no control subject ever diagnosed psychosis, whereas in the experimental groups, diagnoses of psychosis were made by 60 percent of the psychiatrists, 28 percent of the clinical psychologists, and 11 percent of the graduate students.

TABLE 2

DIAGNOSES OF EXPERIMENTAL SUBJECTS

	Mental Illness		
	Psychosis	Neuroses and character disorders	Mental Health
Psychiatrists (N = 25)	15	10	0
Clinical psychologists (N = 25)	7	15	3
Graduate students in clinical psychology (N = 45)	5	35	5

$x^1 = 20.21, df = 4, p < .001.$

Differences between experimental groups are significant at the .001 level, indicating a relationship between the effect of prestige suggestion and professional identity. Prestige suggestion had the most effect upon psychiatrists, biasing them in the direction of psychosis, and the least effect upon graduate students; clinical psychologists fell between these extremes, and both of these groups made significantly more diagnoses of neurosis and health than did the psychiatrists. That this finding is a relationship between prestige suggestion and professional identity, rather than exclusively an occupational hazard of psychiatry, seems logical because psychologists and psychiatrists in the control groups did not diagnose differently. For example, when the prestige confederate of control group 2 said, "You know, I think this is a very rare person, a perfectly healthy man," psychologists, psychiatrists, and graduate students agreed unanimously. That professional identity, rather than length of training or experience, is the relevant variable is illustrated by a within-group analysis: no relationship was found between diagnosis and length of training for any experimental group.

The most common diagnoses of psychosis were, in order, these subclassifications of schizophrenia: pseudoneurotic, ambulatory, paranoid, and hebephrenic. The most common diagnoses of neurosis were, in order, obsessive-compulsive neurosis, hysteria, and passive-aggressive character disorder.

When asked to report the observations on which their diagnosis was based, the only subjects who even approximated doing so were those whose diagnoses were correct. Most subjects either mixed inferences and observations or reported inferences exclusively; some subjects reported inferences labeled as observations. In other words, in spite of explicit instructions to avoid inferences and to be descriptive, only the few subjects who diagnosed health reported such observations as "the patient said that he was enjoying life, said that he was happily married, said that he was effective and productive in his work, and that he had had a happy childhood." And, to illustrate an appropriate connection of inference to observation, only the accurate diagnosticians added such inferences as "he also *seemed* to talk logically, coherently, and in a relaxed manner, and to establish a warm, friendly relationship with the clinician." It therefore was not surprising that no subject changed his diagnosis to one of health after writing a clinical report, although changes between categories of pathology were numerous.

The problem of obtaining consistent agreement between different observers is one of the oldest and most difficult problems of psychological research. This chronic difficulty probably was exacerbated by both the prestige suggestion and the nature of the concept of mental illness itself. That is, mental illness is a mentalistic concept; neurosis and psychosis are never directly observable but must be inferred from behavioral symptoms. This characteristic of the concept may have biased subjects to be inferential rather than descriptive. One psychiatrist illustrated this point by defending his diagnosis of psychosis with the comment, "Of course he looked healthy, but hell, most people are a little neurotic, and who can accept appearances at face value anyway?"

DISCUSSION

Though psychiatric categories may be useful in clinical practice, numerous studies have found them to be unreliable statistically. Different psychiatrists frequently classify the same person within different categories, and the behavioral characteristics of the person may not be predicted from a knowledge of his psychiatric category (5). Furthermore, the same behavior may be considered evidence of mental illness when it occurs in a member of the lower socioeconomic classes and personal idiosyncrasy in a member of the upper class (2). This study suggests that suggestion effects may contribute to the unreliability of psychiatric diagnosis; no control subject ever diagnosed psychosis, for example, though 60 percent of the psychiatrists diagnosed psychosis when this suggestion was present. The following factors may have contributed to the increased effect of the prestige suggestion upon psychiatrists.

1. Psychiatrists are, first and foremost, physicians. It is characteristic of physicians in diagnostically uncertain situations to follow the implicit rule "when in doubt, diagnose illness," because this is a less dangerous error than diagnosing health when illness is in fact present (3).

2. Psychiatry, as a division of organized medicine, has highly differentiated status and role hierarchies, and the system may reward conformity with prestige figures. Psychologists, with historical origins in philosophy and current identifications as social scientists, are more critical and skeptical, even to the point of divisiveness (1), as illustrated by the heterogeneous divisions of the American Psychological Association. The joke "wherever there are two psychologists, there are three opinions" is less descriptive of psychiatrists.

3. In their daily work the psychiatrists probably encountered more psychotics than did clinical psychologists or graduate students, and, thus, they may have expected a psychotic even before the prestige suggestion.

The demonstrated susceptibility of psychiatric diagnosis to distortion through prestige suggestion could be determined in part by the nature of the concept of mental illness itself. It is doubtful that prestige suggestion could bias medical diagnosis so dramatically, on the theory that the substantive reality of physical illness would counterbalance the distorting effects of prestige suggestion. Such substantive realities are absent in mental illness, according to the provocative reasoning of Szasz (4).

Szasz maintains that psychiatric categories are not classifications of diseases, but instead are labels applied to disorganized social behavior. In other words, there is no such natural phenomenon as a disease of the mind; people who exhibit unacceptable social behavior are simply labeled mentally ill. If Szasz is correct, psychiatric diagnosis is inherently unreliable because instead of classifying observable diseases that exist "out there," it would be a process of labeling social behavior in terms of the ethical and social norms of society and psychiatry. Since such norms are vague, vary with culture and socioeconomic class, and are usually not explicit, diagnosis *as labeling* would have to vary with the personal values and perceptual consistencies of the individual diagnostician. From Szasz's viewpoint, diagnosis would be a process of understanding a unique person in a particular life situation, in order to be of help; and psychotherapy is not treatment for disease but a process of learning more effective means of relating to oneself and to other persons.

Although most studies demonstrate the low reliability of psychiatric diagnosis (5), Szasz's point of view lacks general acceptance among mental health professionals. As one subject put it during the debriefing, "God-dammit, the people are in the mental hospitals, and you can't get them out by logic." Such reasoning, however pragmatic, attributes more validity to diagnostic procedures than may be warranted, because sensory or social isolation may produce the symptoms commonly attributed to mental illness. The problems raised by Szasz's provocative reasoning thus remain unsolved. The basic problem in testing Szasz's position experimentally is the difficulty of separating *diagnoses* of mental illness from mental illness itself, if it exists, because there is no operational criterion of mental illness which is independent of psychiatric diagnosis, and with which psychiatric diagnosis might be correlated in a validity study.

This study demonstrates that psychiatric diagnosis may be studied *as if* it were a process of labeling social behavior by manipulating the interpersonal context in which diagnoses are made and by observing changes in the diagnostic labels applied to a person of standard stimulus value. Through such studies, the interpersonal influences that affect psychiatric diagnosis may be better understood, and this increased awareness can only enhance the accuracy and helpfulness of clinical judgment.

REFERENCES

1. Chein, I. Some sources of divisiveness among psychologists. Amer. Psychol., 22: 333–42, 1966.

2. Hollingshead, A. and Redlich, F. *Social Class and Mental Illness: A Community Study*. Wiley, New York, 1958.

3. Scheff, T. *Being Mentally Ill: A Sociological Theory*. Aldine, Chicago, 1966.

4. Szasz, T. *The Myth of Mental Illness*. Hoeber-Harper, New York, 1961.

5. Zigler, E. and Phillips, L. Psychiatric diagnosis and symptomatology. In Milton, O., ed. *Behavior Disorders*, pp. 61–74. Lippincott, New York, 1965.

6

ON BEING SANE IN INSANE PLACES

David L. Rosenhan

This final chapter in Part I provides support for the labeling-theory hypothesis that once the label of mental illness has been applied, it is difficult to remove. In this striking study, sane volunteers posing as mental patients feigned symptoms of psychiatric abnormality upon entrance to a mental hospital, but then immediately dropped all pretense. As indicated below, the volunteers found it difficult to leave the hospital. The study also describes related aspects of their treatment that are consonant with labeling theory.

If sanity and insanity exist, how shall we know them?

The question is neither capricious nor itself insane. However much we may be personally convinced that we can tell the normal from the abnormal, the evidence is simply not compelling. It is commonplace, for example, to read about murder trials in which eminent psychiatrists for the defense are contradicted by equally eminent psychiatrists for the prosecution on the matter of the defendant's sanity. More generally, there is a great deal of conflicting data on the reliability, utility, and meaning of such terms as "sanity," "insanity," "mental illness," and "schizophrenia" (1). Finally, as early as 1934 Benedict suggested that normality and abnormality are not universal (2). What is viewed as normal in one culture may be seen as quite aberrant in another. Thus, notions of normality and abnormality may not be quite as accurate as people believe they are.

To raise questions regarding normality and abnormality is in no way to

Portions of these data were presented to colloquiums of the psychology departments at the University of California at Berkeley and at Santa Barbara; the University of Arizona, Tucson; and Harvard University, Cambridge, Massachusetts. I thank W. Mischel, E. Orne, and M. S. Rosenhan for comments on an earlier draft of this manuscript. From *Science*, 179: 250–258, 1973.

question the fact that some behaviors are deviant or odd. Murder is deviant. So, too, are hallucinations. Nor does raising such questions deny the existence of the personal anguish that is often associated with "mental illness." Anxiety and depression exist. Psychological suffering exists. But normality and abnormality, sanity and insanity, and the diagnoses that flow from them may be less substantive than many believe them to be.

At its heart, the question of whether the sane can be distinguished from the insane (and whether degrees of insanity can be distinguished from one another) is a simple matter: do the salient characteristics that lead to diagnoses reside in the patients themselves or in the environments and contexts in which observers find them? From Bleuler, through Kretchmer, through the formulators of the recently revised *Diagnostic and Statistical Manual* of the American Psychiatric Association, the belief has been strong that patients present symptoms, that those symptoms can be categorized, and, implicitly, that the sane are distinguishable from the insane. More recently, however, this belief has been questioned. Based in part on theoretical and anthropological considerations, but also on philosophical, legal, and therapeutic ones, the view has grown that psychological categorization of mental illness is useless at best and downright harmful, misleading, and pejorative at worst. Psychiatric diagnoses, in this view, are in the minds of the observers and are not valid summaries of characteristics displayed by the observed (3–5).

Gains can be made in deciding which of these is more nearly accurate by getting normal people (that is, people who do not have, and have never suffered, symptoms of serious psychiatric disorders) admitted to psychiatric hospitals and then determining whether they were discovered to be sane and, if so, how. If the sanity of such pseudopatients were always detected, there would be prima facie evidence that a sane individual can be distinguished from the insane context in which he is found. Normality (and presumably abnormality) is distinct enough that it can be recognized wherever it occurs, for it is carried within the person. If, on the other hand, the sanity of the pseudopatients were never discovered, serious difficulties would arise for those who support traditional modes of psychiatric diagnosis. Given that the hospital staff was not incompetent, that the pseudopatient had been behaving as sanely as he had been outside of the hospital, and that it had never been previously suggested that he belonged in a psychiatric hospital, such an unlikely outcome would support the view that psychiatric diagnosis betrays little about the patient but much about the environment in which an observer finds him.

This article describes such an experiment. Eight sane people gained secret admission to twelve different hospitals (6). Their diagnostic experiences constitute the data of the first part of this article; the remainder describes their experiences in psychiatric institutions. Too few psychiatrists and psychologists, even those who have worked in such hospitals, know what the experience is like. They rarely talk about it with former patients, perhaps because they distrust information coming from the previously insane. Those who have worked in psychiatric hospitals are likely to have adapted so thoroughly to the settings that they are insensitive to the impact of that experience. And while there have been occasional reports of researchers who submitted themselves to psychiatric hospitalization (7), these researchers have commonly remained in the hospitals for short periods of time, often with the knowledge of the hospital staff. It is difficult to know the extent to which they were treated as patients or as research colleagues. Nevertheless, their reports about the inside of the psychiatric hospital have been valuable. This article extends those efforts.

PSEUDOPATIENTS AND THEIR SETTINGS

The eight pseudopatients were a varied group. One was a psychology graduate student in his twenties. The remaining seven were older and "established"; among them were three psychologists, a pediatrician, a psychiatrist, a painter, and a housewife. Three pseudopatients were women, five were men. All of them used pseudonyms, lest their alleged diagnoses embarrass them later. Those who were in mental health professions alleged another occupation in order to avoid the special attentions that might be accorded by staff, as a matter of courtesy or caution, to ailing colleagues (8). With the exception of myself (I was the first pseudopatient, and my presence was known to the hospital administrator and chief psychologist and, as far as I can tell, to them alone), the presence of pseudopatients and the nature of the research program was not known to the hospital staffs (9).

The settings were similarly varied. In order to generalize the findings, admission into a variety of hospitals was sought. The twelve hospitals in the sample were located in five different states on the East and West coasts. Some were old and shabby, some were quite new. Some were research oriented, others were not. Some had good staff-patient ratios, others were quite understaffed. Only one was a strictly private hospital. All of the others were supported by state or federal funds or, in one instance, by university funds.

After calling the hospital for an appointment, the pseudopatient arrived at the admissions office complaining that he had been hearing voices. Asked what the voices said, he replied that they were often unclear, but as far as he could tell they said "empty," "hollow," and "thud." The voices were unfamiliar and were of the same sex as the pseudopatient. The choice of these symptoms was occasioned by their apparent similarity to existential symptoms. Such symptoms are alleged to arise from painful concerns about the perceived meaninglessness of one's life. It is as if the hallucinating person were saying, "My life is empty and hollow." The choice of these symptoms was also determined by the *absence* of a single report of existential psychoses in the literature.

Beyond alleging the symptoms and falsifying name, vocation, and employment, no further alterations of person, history, or circumstances were made. The significant events of the pseudopatient's life history were presented as they had actually occurred. Relationships with parents and siblings, with spouse and children, and with people at work and in school were described as they were or had been, consistent with the aforementioned exceptions. Frustrations and upsets were described along with joys and satisfactions. These facts are important to remember. If anything, they strongly biased the subsequent results in favor of detecting sanity, for none of their histories or current behaviors were seriously pathological in any way.

Immediately upon admission to the psychiatric ward, the pseudopatient ceased simulating *any* symptoms of abnormality. In some cases, there was a brief period of mild nervousness and anxiety, for none of the pseudopatients really believed that they would be admitted so easily. Indeed, their shared fear was that they would be immediately exposed as frauds and greatly embarrassed. Moreover, many of them had never visited a psychiatric ward; even those who had, nevertheless had some genuine fears about what might happen to them. Their nervousness, then, was quite appropriate to the novelty of the hospital setting, and it abated rapidly.

Apart from that short-lived nervousness, the pseudopatient behaved on the ward as he behaved "normally." The pseudopatient spoke to patients and staff as he might ordinarily. Because there is uncommonly little to do on a psychiatric ward, he attempted to engage others in conversation. When asked by staff how he was feeling, he indicated that he was fine, that he no longer experienced symptoms. He responded to instructions from attendants, to calls for medication (which was not swallowed), and to dining-hall instructions. Beyond such activities as were available to him on the admissions ward, he spent his time writing down his observations about the ward, its patients, and the staff. Initially, these notes were written "secretly," but as it soon became clear that no one much cared, they were subsequently written on standard tablets of paper in such public places as the dayroom. No secret was made of these activities.

The pseudopatient, very much as a true psychiatric patient, entered a hospital with no foreknowledge of when he would be discharged. Each was told that he would have to get out by his own devices, essentially by convincing the staff that he was sane. The psychological stresses associated with hospitalization were considerable, and all but one of the pseudopatients desired to be discharged almost immediately after being admitted. They were, therefore, motivated not only to behave sanely, but to be paragons of cooperation. That their behavior was in no way disruptive is confirmed by nursing reports, which have been obtained on most of the patients. These reports uniformly indicate that the patients were "friendly," "cooperative," and "exhibited no abnormal indications."

THE NORMAL ARE NOT DETECTABLY SANE

Despite their public "show" of sanity, the pseudopatients were never detected. Admitted, except in one case, with a diagnosis of schizophrenia (10), each was discharged with a diagnosis of schizophrenia "in remission." The label "in remission" should in no way be dismissed as a formality, for at no time during any hospitalization had any question been raised about any pseudopatient's simulation. Nor are there any indications in the hospital records that the pseudopatient's status was suspect. Rather, the evidence is strong that once labeled schizophrenic, the pseudopatient was stuck with that label. If the pseudopatient was to be discharged, he must naturally be "in remission"; but he was not sane, nor, in the institution's view, had he ever been sane.

The uniform failure to recognize sanity cannot be attributed to the quality of the hospitals, for although there were considerable variations among them, several are considered excellent. Nor can it be alleged that there was simply not enough time to observe the pseudopatients. Length of hospitalization ranged from 7 to 52 days, with an average of 19 days. The pseudopatients were not, in fact, carefully observed, but this failure clearly speaks more to traditions within psychiatric hospitals than to lack of opportunity.

Finally, it cannot be said that the failure to recognize the pseudopatients' sanity was due to the fact that they were not behaving sanely. Though there was clearly some tension present in all of them, their daily visitors could detect no serious behavioral consequences—nor, indeed, could other patients. It was quite common for the patients to "detect" the pseudopatients' sanity. During the first three hospitalizations, when accurate counts were kept, 35 of a total of 118 patients on the admissions ward voiced their suspicions, some vigorously. "You're not crazy. You're a journalist, or a professor [referring to the continual note taking]. You're checking up on the hospital." While most of the patients were reassured by the pseudopatient's insistence that he had been sick before he came in but was fine now, some continued to believe that the pseudopatient was sane throughout his hospitalization (11). The fact that the patients often recognized normality when staff did not raises important questions.

Failure to detect sanity during the course of hospitalization may be due to the fact that physicians operate with a strong bias toward what statisticians call the type 2 error (5). That is, physicians are more inclined

to call a healthy person sick (a false positive, type 2) than a sick person
healthy (a false negative, type 1). The reasons for this are not hard to find:
it is clearly more dangerous to misdiagnose illness than health. Better to
err on the side of caution, to suspect illness even among the healthy.

But what holds for medicine does not hold equally well for psychiatry.
Medical illnesses, though unfortunate, are not commonly pejorative.
Psychiatric diagnoses, on the contrary, carry with them personal, legal,
and social stigmas (12). It was therefore important to see whether the
tendency toward diagnosing the sane insane could be reversed. The
following experiment was arranged at a research and teaching hospital
whose staff had heard these findings but doubted that such an error could
occur in their hospital. The staff was informed that at some time during
the following three months, one or more pseudopatients would attempt to
be admitted into the psychiatric hospital. Each staff member was asked to
rate each patient who presented himself at admissions or on the ward
according to the likelihood that the patient was a pseudopatient. A
10-point scale was used, with a 1 and 2 reflecting high confidence that the
patient was a pseudopatient.

Judgments were obtained on 193 patients who were admitted for
psychiatric treatment. All staff who had had sustained contact with or
primary responsibility for the patient—attendants, nurses, psychiatrists,
physicians, and psychologists—were asked to make judgments. Forty-one
patients were alleged, with high confidence, to be pseudopatients by at
least one member of the staff. Twenty-three were considered suspect by at
least one psychiatrist. Nineteen were suspected by one psychiatrist *and* one
other staff member. Actually, no genuine pseudopatient (at least from my
group) presented himself during this period.

The experiment is instructive. It indicates that the tendency to
designate sane people as insane can be reversed when the stakes (in this
case, prestige and diagnostic acumen) are high. But what can be said of
the 19 persons who were suspected of being "sane" by one psychiatrist and
another staff member? Were these people truly "sane," or was it rather the
case that in the course of avoiding the type 2 error the staff tended to make
more errors of the first sort—calling the crazy "sane"? There is no way of
knowing. But one thing is certain: any diagnostic process that lends itself
so readily to massive errors of this sort cannot be a very reliable one.

THE STICKINESS
OF PSYCHODIAGNOSTIC LABELS

Beyond the tendency to call the healthy sick—a tendency that accounts
better for diagnostic behavior on admission than it does for such behavior
after a lengthy period of exposure—the data speak to the massive role of

labeling in psychiatric assessment. Having once been labeled schizo-phrenic, there is nothing the pseudopatient can do to overcome the tag. The tag profoundly colors others' perceptions of him and his behavior.

From one viewpoint, these data are hardly surprising, for it has long been known that elements are given meaning by the context in which they occur. Gestalt psychology made this point vigorously, and Asch (13) demonstrated that there are "central" personality traits (such as "warm" versus "cold") that are so powerful that they markedly color the meaning of other information in forming an impression of a given personality (14). "Insane," "schizophrenic," "manic-depressive," and "crazy" are probably among the most powerful of such central traits. Once a person is designated abnormal, all of his other behaviors and characteristics are colored by that label. Indeed, that label is so powerful that many of the pseudopatients' normal behaviors were overlooked entirely or misinter-preted profoundly. Some examples may clarify this issue.

Earlier, I indicated that there were no changes in the pseudopatient's personal history and current status beyond those of name, employment, and, where necessary, vocation. Otherwise, a veridical description of personal history and circumstances was offered. Those circumstances were not psychotic. How were they made consonant with the diagnosis of psychosis? Or were those diagnoses modified in such a way as to bring them into accord with the circumstances of the pseudopatient's life, as described by him?

As far as I can determine, diagnoses were in no way affected by the relative health of the circumstances of a pseudopatient's life. Rather, the reverse occurred: the perception of his circumstances was shaped entirely by the diagnosis. A clear example of such translation is found in the case of a pseudopatient who had had a close relationship with his mother but was rather remote from his father during his early childhood. During adolescence and beyond, however, his father became a close friend, while his relationship with his mother cooled. His present relationship with his wife was characteristically close and warm. Apart from occasional angry exchanges, friction was minimal. The children had rarely been spanked. Surely there is nothing especially pathological about such a history. Indeed, many readers may see a similar pattern in their own experiences, with no markedly deleterious consequences. Observe, however, how such a history was translated in the psychopathological context, this from the case summary prepared after the patient was discharged.

This white 39-year-old male . . . manifests a long history of considerable ambivalence in close relationships, which begins in early childhood. A warm relationship with his mother cools during his adolescence. A distant relationship to his father is described as becoming very intense. Affective stability is absent. His attempts to control emotionality with his wife and children are punctuated by angry outbursts and, in the case of the children, spankings. And while he says that he has several good friends, one senses considerable ambivalence embedded in those relationships also. . . .

The facts of the case were unintentionally distorted by the staff to achieve consistency with a popular theory of the dynamics of a schizophrenic reaction (15). Nothing of an ambivalent nature had been described in relations with parents, spouse, or friends. To the extent that ambivalence could be inferred, it was probably not greater than is found in all human relationships. It is true the pseudopatient's relationships with his parents changed over time, but in the ordinary context that would hardly be remarkable—indeed, it might very well be expected. Clearly, the meaning ascribed to his verbalizations (that is, ambivalence, affective instability) was determined by the diagnosis: schizophrenia. An entirely different meaning would have been ascribed if it were known that the man was "normal."

All pseudopatients took extensive notes publicly. Under ordinary circumstances, such behavior would have raised questions in the minds of observers, as, in fact, it did among patients. Indeed, it seemed so certain that the notes would elicit suspicion that elaborate precautions were taken to remove them from the ward each day. But the precautions proved needless. The closest any staff member came to questioning these notes occurred when one pseudopatient asked his physician what kind of medication he was receiving and began to write down the response. "You needn't write it," he was told gently. "If you have trouble remembering, just ask me again."

If no questions were asked of the pseudopatients, how was their writing interpreted? Nursing records for three patients indicate that the writing was seen as an aspect of their pathological behavior. "Patient engages in writing behavior" was the daily nursing comment on one of the pseudopatients who was never questioned about his writing. Given that the patient is in the hospital, he must be psychologically disturbed. And given that he is disturbed, continual writing must be a behavioral manifestation of that disturbance, perhaps a subset of the compulsive behaviors that are sometimes correlated with schizophrenia.

One tacit characteristic of psychiatric diagnosis is that it locates the sources of aberration within the individual and only rarely within the complex of stimuli that surrounds him. Consequently, behaviors that are stimulated by the environment are commonly misattributed to the patient's disorder. For example, one kindly nurse found a pseudopatient pacing the long hospital corridors. "Nervous, Mr. X?" she asked. "No, bored," he said.

The notes kept by pseudopatients are full of patient behaviors that were misinterpreted by well-intentioned staff. Often enough, a patient would go "berserk" because he had, wittingly or unwittingly, been mistreated by, say, an attendant. A nurse coming upon the scene would rarely inquire even cursorily into the environmental stimuli of the patient's behavior. Rather, she assumed that his upset derived from his pathology, not from his present interactions with other staff members. Occasionally, the staff might assume that the patient's family (especially when they had recently visited) or other patients had stimulated the outburst. But never were the staff found to assume that one of themselves or the structure of the hospital had anything to do with a patient's behavior. One psychiatrist pointed to a group of patients who were sitting outside the cafeteria entrance half an hour before lunchtime. He indicated to a group of young residents that such behavior was characteristic of the oral-acquisitive nature of the syndrome. It did not seem to occur to him that there were very few things to anticipate in a psychiatric hospital besides eating.

A psychiatric label has a life and an influence of its own. Once the impression has been formed that the patient is schizophrenic, the expectation is that he will continue to be schizophrenic. When a sufficient amount of time has passed during which the patient has done nothing bizarre, he is considered to be in remission and available for discharge. But the label endures beyond discharge, with the unconfirmed expectation that he will behave as a schizophrenic again. Such labels, conferred by mental health professionals, are as influential on the patient as they are on his relatives and friends, and it should not surprise anyone that the diagnosis acts on all of them as a self-fulfilling prophecy. Eventually, the patient himself accepts the diagnosis, with all of its surplus meanings and expectations, and he behaves accordingly (5).

The inferences to be made from these matters are quite simple. Much as Zigler and Phillips have demonstrated that there is enormous overlap in the symptoms presented by patients who have been variously diagnosed (16), so there is enormous overlap in the behaviors of the sane and the insane. The sane are not "sane" all of the time. We lose our tempers "for no good reason." We are occasionally depressed or anxious, again for no good reason. And we may find it difficult to get along with one or another person—again for no reason that we can specify. Similarly, the insane are not always insane. Indeed, it was the impression of the pseudopatients while living with them that they were sane for long periods of time—that the bizarre behaviors upon which their diagnoses were allegedly predicated constituted only a small fraction of their total behavior. If it makes no sense to label ourselves permanently depressed on the basis of an occasional depression, then it takes better evidence than is presently available to label all patients insane or schizophrenic on the basis of bizarre behaviors or cognitions. It seems more useful, as Mischel (17) has pointed out, to limit our discussions to *behaviors*, the stimuli that provoke them, and their correlates.

It is not known why powerful impressions of personality traits, such as "crazy" or "insane," arise. Conceivably, when the origins of and stimuli that give rise to a behavior are remote or unknown, or when the behavior strikes us as immutable, trait labels regarding the *behaver* arise. When, on the other hand, the origins and stimuli are known and available, discourse is limited to the behavior itself. Thus, I may hallucinate because I am sleeping, or I may hallucinate because I have ingested a peculiar drug. These are termed sleep-induced hallucinations, or dreams, and drug-induced hallucinations, respectively. But when the stimuli to my hallucinations are unknown, that is called craziness, or schizophrenia—as if that inference were somehow as illuminating as the others.

THE EXPERIENCE
OF PSYCHIATRIC HOSPITALIZATION

The term "mental illness" is of recent origin. It was coined by persons who were humane in their inclinations and who wanted very much to raise the station of (and the public's sympathies toward) the psychologically disturbed from that of witches and "crazies" to one that was akin to the physically ill. And they were at least partially successful, for the treatment of the mentally ill *has* improved considerably over the years. But although treatment has improved, it is doubtful that people really regard the mentally ill in the same way that they view the physically ill. A broken leg is something one recovers from, but mental illness allegedly endures forever (18). A broken leg does not threaten the observer, but a crazy schizophrenic? There is by now a host of evidence that attitudes toward the mentally ill are characterized by fear, hostility, aloofness, suspicion, and dread (19). The mentally ill are society's lepers.

That such attitudes infect the general population is perhaps not surprising, only upsetting. But that they affect the professionals—attendants, nurses, physicians, psychologists, and social workers—who treat and deal with the mentally ill is more disconcerting, both because such attitudes are self-evidently pernicious and because they are unwitting. Most mental health professionals would insist that they are sympathetic toward the mentally ill, that they are neither avoidant nor hostile. But it is more likely that an exquisite ambivalence characterizes their relations with psychiatric patients, such that their avowed impulses are only part of their entire attitude. Negative attitudes are there too and can easily be detected. Such attitudes should not surprise us. They are the natural offspring of the labels patients wear and the places in which they are found.

Consider the structure of the typical psychiatric hospital. Staff and patients are strictly segregated. Staff have their own living space, including their dining facilities, bathrooms, and assembly places. The glassed quarters that contain the professional staff, which the pseudopatients came to call "the cage," sit out on every dayroom. The staff emerge primarily for caretaking purposes—to give medication, to conduct a therapy or group meeting, to instruct or reprimand a patient. Otherwise, staff keep to themselves, almost as if the disorder that afflicts their charges is somehow catching.

So much is patient-staff segregation the rule that in four public hospitals in which an attempt was made to measure the degree to which staff and patients mingle, it was necessary to use "time out of the staff cage" as the operational measure. Though it was not the case that all time spent out of the cage was spent mingling with patients (attendants, for example, would occasionally emerge to watch television in the dayroom), it was the only way in which one could gather reliable data on time for measuring.

The average amount of time spent by attendants outside of the cage was 11.3 percent (range, 3 to 52 percent). This figure does not represent only time spent mingling with patients, but also includes time spent on such chores as folding laundry, supervising patients while they shave, directing ward cleanup, and sending patients to off-ward activities. It was the relatively rare attendant who spent time talking with patients or playing games with them. It proved impossible to obtain a "percent mingling time" for nurses, because the amount of time they spent out of the cage was too brief. Rather, we counted instances of emergence from the cage. On the average, daytime nurses emerged from the cage 11.5 times per shift, including instances when they left the ward entirely (range, 4 to 39 times). Late afternoon and night nurses were even less available, emerging on the average 9.4 times per shift (range, 4 to 41 times). Data on early morning nurses, who arrived usually after midnight and departed at 8 A.M., are not available because patients were asleep during most of this period.

Physicians, especially psychiatrists, were even less available. They were rarely seen on the wards. Quite commonly, they would be seen only when they arrived and departed, with the remaining time being spent in their offices or in the cage. On the average, physicians emerged on the ward 6.7 times per day (range, 1 to 17 times). It proved difficult to make an accurate estimate in this regard, because physicians often maintained hours that allowed them to come and go at different times.

The hierarchical organization of the psychiatric hospital has been commented on before (20), but the latent meaning of that kind of organization is worth noting again. Those with the most power have the least to do with patients, and those with the least power are most involved with them. Recall, however, that the acquisition of role-appropriate behaviors occurs mainly through the observation of others, with the most powerful having the most influence. Consequently, it is understandable that attendants not only spend more time with patients than do any other members of the staff—that is required by their station in the hierarchy—but also, insofar as they learn from their superiors' behavior, spend as little time with patients as they can. Attendants are seen mainly in the cage, which is where the models, the action, and the power are.

I turn now to a different set of studies, these dealing with staff response to patient-initiated contact. It has long been known that the amount of time a person spends with you can be an index of your significance to him. If he initiates and maintains eye contact, there is reason to believe that he is considering your requests and needs. If he pauses to chat or actually stops and talks, there is added reason to infer that he is individuating you. In four hospitals, the pseudopatient approached the staff member with a request that took the following form: "Pardon me, Mr. [or Dr. or Mrs.] X, could you tell me when I will be eligible for grounds privileges?" (or ". . . when I will be presented at the staff meeting?" or ". . . when I am likely to be discharged?"). Though the content of the question varied according to the appropriateness of the target and the pseudopatient's (apparent) current needs, the form was always a courteous and relevant request for information. Care was taken never to approach a particular member of the staff more than once a day, lest the staff member become suspicious or irritated. In examining these data, remember that the behavior of the pseudopatients was neither bizarre nor disruptive. One could indeed engage in good conversation with them.

The data for these experiments are shown in Table 1, separately for physicians (column 1) and for nurses and attendants (column 2). Minor differences among these four institutions were overwhelmed by the degree to which staff avoided continuing contacts that patients had initiated. By far, their most common response consisted of either a brief response to the question, offered while they were "on the move" and with head averted, or no response at all.

The encounter frequently took the following bizarre form. Pseudopatient: "Pardon me, Dr. X. Could you tell me when I am eligible for grounds privileges?" Physician: "Good morning, Dave. How are you today?" (Moves off without waiting for a response.)

It is instructive to compare these data with data recently obtained at Stanford University. It has been alleged that large and eminent universities are characterized by faculty who are so busy that they have no time for students. For this comparison, a young lady approached individual faculty members who seemed to be walking purposefully to some meeting or teaching engagement and asked them the following six questions.

1. "Pardon me, could you direct me to Encina Hall?" (At the medical school: ". . . to the Clinical Research Center?")

2. "Do you know where Fish Annex is?" (There is no Fish Annex at Stanford.)

3. "Do you teach here?"

TABLE 1

SELF-INITIATED CONTACT BY PSEUDOPATIENTS WITH PSYCHIATRISTS AND
NURSES AND ATTENDANTS, COMPARED WITH CONTACT WITH OTHER GROUPS.

| | Psychiatric hospitals | | University campus (nonmedical) | University medical center | | |
| | | | | Physicians | | |
Contact	(1) Psychiatrists	(2) Nurses and attendants	(3) Faculty	(4) "Looking for a psychiatrist"	(5) "Looking for an internist"	(6) No additional comment
Responses						
Moves on, head averted (%)	71	88	0	0	0	0
Makes eye contact (%)	23	10	0	11	0	0
Pauses and chats (%)	2	2	0	11	0	10
Stops and talks (%)	4	0.5	100	78	100	90
Mean number of questions answered (out of 6)	*	*	6	3.8	4.8	4.5
Respondents (number)	13	47	14	18	15	10
Attempts (number)	185	1283	14	18	15	10

* Not applicable.

4. "How does one apply for admission to the college?" (At the medical school: ". . . to the medical school?")
5. "Is it difficult to get in?"
6. "Is there financial aid?"

Without exception, as can be seen in Table 1 (column 3), all of the questions were answered. No matter how rushed they were, all respondents not only maintained eye contact but also stopped to talk. Indeed, many of the respondents went out of their way to direct or take the questioner to the office she was seeking, to try to locate "Fish Annex," or to discuss with her the possibilities of being admitted to the university.

Similar data, also shown in Table 1 (columns 4, 5, and 6), were obtained in the hospital. Here too, the young lady came prepared with six questions. After the first question, however, she remarked to 18 of her respondents (column 4), "I'm looking for a psychiatrist," and to 15 others (column 5), "I'm looking for an internist." Ten other respondents received no inserted comment (column 6). The general degree of cooperative responses is considerably higher for these university groups than it was for pseudopatients in psychiatric hospitals. Even so, differences are apparent within the medical school setting. Once having indicated that she was looking for a psychiatrist, the degree of cooperation elicited was less than when she sought an internist.

POWERLESSNESS AND DEPERSONALIZATION

Eye contact and verbal contact reflect concern and individuation; their absence, avoidance and depersonalization. The data I have presented do not do justice to the rich daily encounters that grew up around matters of depersonalization and avoidance. I have records of patients who were beaten by staff for the sin of having initiated verbal contact. During my own experience, for example, one patient was beaten in the presence of other patients for having approached an attendant and told him, "I like you." Occasionally, punishment meted out to patients for misdemeanors seemed so excessive that it could not be justified by the most radical interpretations of psychiatric canon. Nevertheless, they appeared to go unquestioned. Tempers were often short. A patient who had not heard a call for medication would be roundly excoriated, and the morning attendants would often wake patients with, "Come on, you m——f——s, out of bed!"

Neither anecdotal nor "hard" data can convey the overwhelming sense of powerlessness that invades the individual as he is continually exposed to the depersonalization of the psychiatric hospital. It hardly matters *which* psychiatric hospital—the excellent public ones and the very plush private hospital were better than the rural and shabby ones in this regard, but, again, the features that psychiatric hospitals had in common overwhelmed by far their apparent differences.

Powerlessness was evident everywhere. The patient is deprived of many of his legal rights by dint of his psychiatric commitment (21). He is shorn of credibility by virtue of his psychiatric label. His freedom of movement is restricted. He cannot initiate contact with the staff, but may only respond to such overtures as they make. Personal privacy is minimal. Patient quarters and possessions can be entered and examined by any staff member, for whatever reason. His personal history and anguish is available to any staff member (often including the "grey lady" and "candy striper" volunteer) who chooses to read his folder, regardless of their therapeutic relationship to him. His personal hygiene and waste evacuation are often monitored. The water closets may have no doors.

At times, depersonalization reached such proportions that pseudopatients had the sense that they were invisible, or at least unworthy of account. Upon being admitted, I and other pseudopatients took the initial physical examinations in a semipublic room, where staff members went about their own business as if we were not there.

On the ward, attendants delivered verbal and occasionally serious physical abuse to patients in the presence of other observing patients, some of whom (the pseudopatients) were writing it all down. Abusive behavior terminated quite abruptly, however, when other staff members were known to be coming. Staff are credible witnesses. Patients are not.

A nurse unbuttoned her uniform to adjust her brassiere in the presence of an entire ward of viewing men. One did not have the sense that she was being seductive. Rather, she didn't notice us. A group of staff persons might point to a patient in the dayroom and discuss him animatedly, as if he were not there.

One illuminating instance of depersonalization and invisibility occurred with regard to medications. All told, the pseudopatients were administered nearly 2,100 pills, including Elavil, Stelazine, Compazine, and Thorazine, to name but a few. (That such a variety of medications should have been administered to patients presenting identical symptoms is itself worthy of note.) Only two were swallowed. The rest were either pocketed or deposited in the toilet. The pseudopatients were not alone in this. Although I have no precise records of how many patients rejected their medications, the pseudopatients frequently found the medications of other patients in the toilet before they deposited their own. As long as they were cooperative, their behavior and that of the pseudopatients in this matter, as in other important matters, went unnoticed throughout.

Reactions to such depersonalization among pseudopatients were intense. Although they had come to the hospital as participant observers and were fully aware that they did not "belong," they nevertheless found themselves caught up in and fighting the process of depersonalization.

Some examples: a graduate student in psychology asked his wife to bring his textbooks to the hospital so he could "catch up on his homework"—this despite the elaborate precautions taken to conceal his professional association. The same student, who had trained for quite some time to get into the hospital, and who had looked forward to the experience, "remembered" some drag races that he had wanted to see on the weekend and insisted that he be discharged by that time. Another pseudopatient attempted a romance with a nurse. Subsequently, he informed the staff that he was applying for admission to graduate school in psychology and was very likely to be admitted, since a graduate professor was one of his regular hospital visitors. The same person began to engage in psychotherapy with other patients—all of this as a way of becoming a person in an impersonal environment.

THE SOURCES OF DEPERSONALIZATION

What are the origins of depersonalization? I have already mentioned two. The first are attitudes held by all of us toward the mentally ill—including those who treat them—attitudes characterized by fear, distrust, and horrible expectations on one hand, and benevolent intentions on the other. Our ambivalence leads, in this instance as in others, to avoidance.

Second, and not entirely separate from the first, the hierarchical structure of the psychiatric hospital facilitates depersonalization. Those who are at the top have the least to do with patients, and their behavior inspires the rest of the staff. Average daily contact with psychiatrists, psychologists, residents, and physicians—combined—ranged from 3.9 to 25.1 minutes, with an overall mean of 6.8 (six pseudopatients over a total of 129 days of hospitalization). Included in this average are time spent in the admissions interview, ward meetings in the presence of a senior staff member, group and individual psychotherapy contacts, case presentation conferences, and discharge meetings. Clearly, patients do not spend much time in interpersonal contact with doctoral staff. And doctoral staff serve as models for nurses and attendants.

There are probably other sources. Psychiatric installations are presently in serious financial straits. Staff shortages are pervasive, staff time at a premium. Something has to give, and that something is patient contact. Yet, although financial stresses are realities, too much can be made of them. I have the impression that the psychological forces that result in depersonalization are much stronger than the fiscal ones and that the addition of more staff would not correspondingly improve patient care in this regard. The incidence of staff meetings and the enormous amount of record keeping on patients, for example, have not been reduced as substantially as has patient contact. Priorities exist, even during hard times. Patient contact is not a significant priority in the traditional psychiatric hospital, and fiscal pressures do not account for this. Avoidance and depersonalization may.

Heavy reliance upon psychotropic medication tacitly contributes to depersonalization by convincing staff that treatment is indeed being conducted and that further patient contact may not be necessary. Even here, however, caution needs to be exercised in understanding the role of psychotropic drugs. If patients were powerful rather than powerless, if they were viewed as interesting individuals rather than as diagnostic entities, if they were socially significant rather than social lepers, if their anguish truly and wholly compelled our sympathies and concerns, would we not *seek* contact with them, despite the availability of medications? Perhaps for the pleasure of it all?

THE CONSEQUENCES
OF LABELING AND DEPERSONALIZATION

Whenever the ratio of what is known to what needs to be known approaches zero, we tend to invent "knowledge" and assume that we understand more than we actually do. We seem unable to acknowledge that we simply don't know. The needs for diagnosis and remediation of behavioral and emotional problems are enormous. But rather than acknowledge that we are just embarking on understanding, we continue to label patients "schizophrenic," "manic-depressive," and "insane," as if in those words we had captured the essence of understanding. The facts of the matter are that we have known for a long time that diagnoses are often not useful or reliable, but we have nevertheless continued to use them. We now know that we cannot distinguish insanity from sanity. It is depressing to consider how that information will be used.

Not merely depressing, but frightening. How many people, one wonders, are sane but not recognized as such in our psychiatric institutions? How many have been needlessly stripped of their privileges of citizenship, from the rights to vote, to drive, and to handle their own accounts? How many have feigned insanity in order to avoid the criminal consequences of their behavior, and, conversely, how many would rather stand trial than live interminably in a psychiatric hospital—but are wrongly thought to be mentally ill? How many have been stigmatized by well-intentioned but nevertheless erroneous diagnoses? On the last point, recall again that a "type 2 error" in psychiatric diagnosis does not have the same consequences it does in medical diagnosis. A diagnosis of cancer that has been found to be in error is cause for celebration. But psychiatric diagnoses are rarely found to be in error. The label sticks, a mark of inadequacy forever.

Finally, how many patients might be "sane" outside the psychiatric hospital but seem insane in it—not because craziness resides in them, as it were, but because they are responding to a bizarre setting, one that may be unique to institutions that harbor nether people? Goffman (4) calls the process of socialization to such institutions "mortification"—an apt metaphor that includes the processes of depersonalization that have been described here. And though it is impossible to know whether the pseudopatients' responses to these processes are characteristic of all inmates—they were, after all, not real patients—it is difficult to believe that these processes of socialization to a psychiatric hospital provide useful attitudes or habits of response for living in the "real world."

SUMMARY AND CONCLUSIONS

It is clear that we cannot distinguish the sane from the insane in psychiatric hospitals. The hospital itself imposes a special environment in which the meanings of behavior can easily be misunderstood. The consequences to patients hospitalized in such an environment—the powerlessness, depersonalization, segregation, mortification, and self-labeling—seem undoubtedly countertherapeutic.

I do not, even now, understand this problem well enough to perceive solutions. But two matters seem to offer some promise. The first concerns the proliferation of community mental health facilities, of crisis intervention centers, of the human potential movement, and of behavior therapies that, for all of their own problems, tend to avoid psychiatric labels, to focus on specific problems and behaviors, and to retain the individual in a relatively nonpejorative environment. Clearly, to the extent that we refrain from sending the distressed to insane places, our impressions of them are less likely to be distorted. (The risk of distorted perceptions, it seems to me, is always present, because we are much more sensitive to an individual's behaviors and verbalizations than we are to the subtle contextual stimuli that often promote them. At issue here is a matter of magnitude. And, as I have shown, the magnitude of distortion is exceedingly high in the extreme context of a psychiatric hospital.)

The second matter that might prove promising speaks to the need to increase the sensitivity of mental health workers and researchers to the *Catch-22* position of psychiatric patients. Simply reading materials in this area will help some such workers and researchers. For others, directly experiencing the impact of psychiatric hospitalization will be of enormous use. Clearly, further research into the social psychology of such total institutions will both facilitate treatment and deepen understanding.

I and the other pseudopatients in the psychiatric setting had distinctly negative reactions. We do not pretend to describe the subjective experiences of true patients. Theirs may be different from ours, particularly with the passage of time and the necessary process of adaptation to one's environment. But we can and do speak to the relatively more objective indexes of treatment within the hospital. It could be a mistake, and a very unfortunate one, to consider that what happened to us derived from malice or stupidity on the part of the staff. Quite the contrary, our overwhelming impression of them was of people who really cared, who were committed, and who were uncommonly intelligent. Where they failed, as they sometimes did painfully, it would be more accurate to attribute those failures to the environment in which they, too, found themselves than to personal callousness. Their perceptions and behavior were controlled by the situation, rather than being motivated by a malicious disposition. In a more benign environment, one that was less attached to global diagnosis, their behaviors and judgments might have been more benign and effective.

REFERENCES

1. P. Ash, *J. Abnorm. Soc. Psychol.* **44**, 272 (1949); A. T. Beck, *Amer. J. Psychiat.* **119**, 210 (1962); A. T. Boisen, *Psychiatry* **2**, 233 (1938); N. Kreitman, *J. Ment. Sci.* **107**, 876 (1961); N. Kreitman, P. Sainsbury, J. Morrisey, J. Towers, J. Scrivener, *J. Ment. Sci.* **107**, 887 (1961); H. O. Schmitt and C. P. Fonda, *J. Abnorm. Soc. Psychol.* **52**, 262 (1956); W. Seeman, *J. Nerv. Ment. Dis.* **118**, 541 (1953). For an analysis of these artifacts and summaries of the disputes, see J. Zubin, *Annu. Rev. Psychol.* **18**, 373 (1967); and L. Phillips and J. G. Draguns, *Annu. Rev. Psychol.* **22**, 447 (1971).

2. R. Benedict, *J. Gen. Psychol.* **10**, 59 (1934).

3. See in this regard H. Becker, *Outsiders: Studies in the Sociology of Deviance* (Free Press, New York, 1963); B. M. Braginsky, D. D. Braginsky, K. Ring, *Methods of Madness: The Mental Hospital as a Last Resort* (Holt, Rinehart & Winston, New York, 1969); G. M. Crocetti and P. V. Lemkau, *Amer. Sociol. Rev.* **30**, 577 (1965); E. Goffmann, *Behavior in Public Places* (Free Press, New York, 1964); R. D. Laing, *The Divided Self: A Study of Sanity and Madness* (Quadrangle, Chicago, 1960); D. L. Phillips, *Amer. Sociol. Rev.* **28**, 963 (1963); T. R. Sarbin, *Psychol. Today* **6**, 18 (1972); E. Schur, *Amer. J. Sociol.* **75**, 309 (1969); T. Szasz, *Law, Liberty, and Psychiatry* (Macmillan, New York, 1963); T. Szasz, *The Myth of Mental Illness: Foundations of a Theory of Mental Illness* (Hoeber-Harper, New York, 1963). For a critique of some of these views, see W. R. Gove, *Amer. Sociol. Rev.* **35**, 873 (1970).

4. E. Goffman, *Asylums* (Doubleday, Garden City, N.Y., 1961).

5. T. J. Scheff, *Being Mentally Ill: A Sociological Theory* (Aldine, Chicago, 1966).

6. Data from a ninth pseudopatient are not incorporated in this report because, although his sanity went undetected, he falsified aspects of his personal history, including his marital status and parental relationships. His experimental behaviors therefore were not identical with those of the other pseudopatients.

7. A. Barry, *Bellevue Is a State of Mind* (Harcourt Brace Jovanovich, New York, 1971); I. Belknap, *Human Problems of a State Mental Hospital* (McGraw-Hill, New York, 1956); W. Caudill, F. C. Redlich, H. R. Gilmore, E. B. Brody, *Amer. J. Orthopsychiat.* **22**, 314 (1952); A. R. Goldman, R. H. Bohr, T. A. Steinberg, *Prof. Psychol.* **1**, 427 (1970); unauthored, *Roche Report* 1 (No. 13), 8 (1971).

8. Beyond the personal difficulties that the pseudopatient is likely to experience in the hospital, there are legal and social ones that, combined, require considerable attention before entry. For example, once admitted to a psychiatric institution, it is difficult, if not impossible, to be discharged on short notice, state law to the contrary notwithstanding. I was not sensitive to these difficulties at the outset of the project, nor to the personal and situational emergencies that can arise, but later a writ of *habeas corpus* was prepared for each of the entering pseudopatients and an attorney was kept on call during every hospitalization. I am grateful to John Kaplan and Robert Bartels for legal advice and assistance in these matters.

9. However distasteful such concealment is, it was a necessary first step to examining these questions. Without concealment, there would have been no way to know how valid these experiences were; nor was there any way of knowing whether whatever detections occurred were a tribute to the diagnostic acumen of the staff or to the hospital's rumor network. Obviously, since my concerns are general ones that cut across individual hospitals and staffs, I have respected their anonymity and have eliminated clues that might lead to their identification.

10. Interestingly, of the twelve admissions, eleven were diagnosed as schizophrenic and one, with the identical symptomatology, as manic-depressive psychosis. This diagnosis has a more favorable prognosis, and it was given by the only private hospital in our sample. On the relations between social class and psychiatric diagnosis, see A. de B. Hollingshead and F. C. Redlich, *Social Class and Mental Illness: A Community Study* (John Wiley, New York, 1958).

11. It is possible, of course, that patients have quite broad latitudes in diagnosis and therefore are inclined to call many people sane, even those whose behavior is patently aberrant. However, although we have no hard data on this matter, it was our distinct impression that this was not the case. In many instances, patients not only singled us out for attention, but came to imitate our behaviors and styles.

12. J. Cumming and E. Cumming, *Community Ment. Health* **1**, 135 (1965); A. Farina and K. Ring, *J. Abnorm. Psychol.* **70**, 47 (1965); H. E. Freeman and O. G. Simmons, *The Mental Patient Comes Home* (John Wiley, New York, 1963); W. J. Johannsen, *Ment. Hygiene* **53**, 218 (1969); A. S. Linsky, *Soc. Psychiat.* **5**, 166 (1970).

13. S. E. Asch, *J. Abnorm. Soc. Psychol.* **41**, 258 (1946); *Social Psychology* (Prentice-Hall, New York, 1952).

14. See also I. N. Mensh and J. Wishner, *J. Personality* **16**, 188 (1947); J. Wishner, *Psychol. Rev.* **67**, 96 (1960); J. S. Bruner and R. Tagiuri, in *Handbook of Social Psychology*, G. Lindzey, Ed. (Addison-Wesley, Cambridge, Mass., 1954), vol. 2, pp. 634–654; J. S. Bruner, D. Shapiro, R. Tagiuri, in *Person Perception and Interpersonal Behavior*, R. Tagiuri and L. Petrullo, Eds. (Stanford University Press, Stanford, Calif., 1958), pp. 277–288.

15. For an example of a similar self-fulfilling prophecy, in this instance dealing

with the "central" trait of intelligence, see R. Rosenthal and L. Jacobson, *Pygmalion in the Classroom* (Holt, Rinehart & Winston, New York, 1968).

16. E. Zigler and L. Phillips, *J. Abnorm. Soc. Psychol.* **63,** 69 (1961). See also R. K. Freudenberg and J. P. Robertson, *A.M.A. Arch. Neurol. Psychiatr.* **76,** 14 (1956).

17. W. Mischel, *Personality and Assessment* (John Wiley, New York, 1968).

18. The most recent and unfortunate instance of this tenet is that of Senator Thomas Eagleton.

19. T. R. Sarbin and J. C. Mancuso, *J. Clin. Consult. Psychol.* **35,** 159 (1970); T. R. Sarbin, *J. Clin. Consult. Psychol.* **31,** 447 (1967); J. C. Nunnally, Jr., *Popular Conceptions of Mental Health* (Holt, Rinehart & Winston, New York, 1961).

20. A. H. Stanton and M. S. Schwartz, *The Mental Hospital: A Study of Institutional Participation in Psychiatric Illness and Treatment* (Basic Books, New York, 1954).

21. D. B. Wexler and S. E. Scoville, *Ariz. Law Rev.* **13,** 1 (1971).

PART II
Changing the System: Some Explorations

7

LABELING, EMOTION, AND INDIVIDUAL CHANGE

Thomas J. Scheff

Chapter 7, an essay written especially for this volume, introduces a new idea into labeling theory: if the social system of labeling is to be changed, we must seek its roots not only in the social structure but also in the individual psychology of the labelers. One important root, it is argued, is in the systematic repression of emotions. The chapter then discusses some possible avenues for decreasing emotional repression and thereby, hopefully, labeling. Emphasis is placed on the discharge of repressed emotion in social settings.

The purpose of this chapter is to discuss some issues concerning the labeling of mental illness. I will seek to define labeling as a process of human behavior, and to relate this process to areas of life that do not involve deviance. In particular, I will seek to place labeling in the larger social context in which it takes place, with emphasis on its psychological context and its relationship to individual change. In this discussion I will look for ways to resolve two problems. The first concerns formulating an explicit definition of deviance as a process. The second problem is to relate this process to basic sociological and psychological concepts.

Labeling theory is a sociologistic theory, in that it deals only with social processes. It provides a vantage point for generating new ideas about the nature of mental illness and its relationship to social structure. Yet it should be obvious that labeling theory is itself biased. It is a simple linear

My thanks to Richard Appelbaum, Richard Flacks, and Morton Schatzman for their comments on an earlier draft of this chapter.

theory of a complex, convoluted area of human experience. This linear theory is as useful as it is because it contradicts exactly the linear theory that prevails in most research on mental illness—the medical model. That is, labeling theory is the antithesis of the medical model thesis and, as such, is extraordinarily helpful in obtaining a fresh look at a difficult subject matter.

But it is also true that labeling theory is not a synthesis. As the theory stands now, it is difficult to see its relationship—although it is a sociologistic theory—with other sociological theories, much less with psychological theories of behavior. Several studies of mental illness have indicated the need for a theory that would integrate both individual and collective behavior.[1] In this chapter, I will seek to broaden labeling theory so that its relationships with other sociological and psychological theories might become clearer. I will place particular emphasis upon relating the theory to a theory of individual change.

The basic variable in labeling theory is the dichotomy between labeling and denial. One source of difficulty with the theory is that the variable itself has never been defined. That is, only the extremes, labeling and denial, have been defined. The labeling pole of the variable has been represented by the public event in which an individual is denounced by an authority as being essentially a deviant.[2] At the other pole, denial is seen as the ignoring or rationalizing of behavior that in other contexts could be defined as deviant. For practical purposes in research on labeling, public, official denunciations such as criminal conviction or civil commitment of the mentally ill have been taken as examples of labeling, and any reaction short of this—such as informal handling of illegal acts by policemen, or private psychiatric treatment of persons thought to be mentally ill—has been seen as denial. Obviously, lesser reactions such as rationalizing ("Boys will be boys," "It could happen to anyone") or totally ignoring the illicit behavior, are also seen as examples of denial. How can we define the continuum of which these two poles are the extremes?

The key to the labeling-denial continuum, it seems to me, is the process of defining a person as essentially and *only* a deviant. Compare the attitude of denial contained in the description, "George drinks like a fish, but he is a talented, compassionate, and accomplished man," with the attitude of labeling expressed in the statement, "George is nothing but a drunk." The attitude of labeling is to reduce a complex individual with many attributes and an eventful biography to a single descriptive trait. A person is defined exclusively by some single aspect of his character or behavior.

[1] See, for example, my study, "Users and Non-users of a Student Psychiatric Clinic," *Journal of Health and Human Behavior*, 7 (1966), 114–21; and Arnold S. Linsky, "Community Homogeneity and Exclusion of the Mentally Ill: Rejection Versus Consensus about Deviance," *Journal of Health and Social Behavior*, 11 (1970), 304–11.

[2] Harold Garfinkel, "Conditions of Successful Degradation Ceremonies," *American Journal of Sociology*, 61 (1956), 420–24.

The process of labeling may be seen as giving rise to a master status that excludes all other statuses from consideration. The fact that a person is a "criminal"—that is, convicted of a felony—may cause others to ignore all of his other statuses (male, father, husband, uncle, real estate broker, neighbor, Mason, and so on). The deviant role obscures and in some instances supersedes all other roles.

CATEGORIZATION OF PERSONS

The variable of labeling and denial can be defined as the degree of categorization—the degree to which a complex human being is reduced to a single category. Given this definition, we can more clearly see the relationship of labeling and denial to the larger context in which it occurs. Categorization of persons is a pervasive, indeed ubiquitous process in modern society. The degree of categorization that occurs in human activities is a crucial characteristic of a whole society, not just in the area of deviance but in most areas of human affairs.

What I mean here by categorization is not merely the mental operation of abstracting one element from some complex reality, as in the process of classification. Such a mental process is often necessary and desirable, and is, in fact, the basis for abstract thought. Categorization, as I conceive of it here, includes two further steps beyond this mental process: first, forgetting that the category is an abstraction; second, *acting* as if the abstraction were the thing itself.

In this sense, categorization of persons is akin to the Marxian concept of reification. Berger and Pullberg, for example, state in their discussion of reification that

alienation is the process by which man forgets that the world he lives in has been produced by himself. . . . By reification we mean the moment in the process of alienation in which the characteristic of thing-hood becomes the standard of objective reality.[3]

In light of this discussion, labeling can be seen as a particular kind of categorization—the categorization of deviants—just as categorization, in turn, can be considered a special case of reification—the reification of persons.

The analysis of the conditions that give rise to the categorization of persons, and the consequences of such categorization, constitute a substantial chapter of the literature in the social sciences. Various aspects of this problem are considered in distinctions such as the following: *gemeinschaft* versus *gesellschaft* (Toennies), unalienated versus alienated

---

[3] Peter Berger and Stanley Pullberg, "Reification and the Sociological Critique of Consciousness," *History and Theory*, 4, no. 2 (1965), 196–211.

labor (Marx), status versus contract (Henry Maine), mechanical versus organic solidarity (Durkheim), community versus bureaucracy (Weber), primary versus secondary relations (Cooley), folk versus urban (Redfield), and person versus role (Linton).

The most comprehensive of these discussions, and the one that relates most directly to the labeling-denial continuum, is Martin Buber's treatment of I-thou and I-it relationships.[4] According to Buber, an I-thou relationship is one in which each person treats the other as a sapient being like himself; in an I-it relationship, in contrast, each person treats the other as an object, as a means to an end rather than as an end in himself.

Buber sees bureaucracy as constituting an important example of I-it relationships. In a bureaucratic setting, individuals react to one another in terms of their organizational function rather than as individuals. An even more extreme example of I-it relationships is provided by typical reactions of collectivities to enemies, strangers, and deviants. Such individuals may be used, segregated, or slaughtered without compunction, for the members of the collectivity often do not personify them as human beings like themselves. The characteristic language in these confrontations—for instance, "murderous beasts," "filthy vermin," "scum of the earth"— establishes that such outsiders are personified not as human beings but as animals, insects, or objects.

Although I-it relationships are characteristic of contacts within bureaucracies, they are also found, Buber indicates, in many interpersonal relationships that we suppose to be intimate and personal. Relationships between parents and children or between husbands and wives may be based upon each individual personifying the other as something less than a fully conscious individual like himself. Thus, the man who sees a woman as a sex object, the wife who sees her husband merely as the breadwinner, or the child who sees his parents only as a source of authoritative commands is involved in an I-it relationship as much as the parent who sees his child only as a possible source of prestige or honor.[5]

According to Buber, the essential element in an I-thou relationship that differentiates it from all other relationships is that one person is *present* for the other. One is present when he is sensitive to the other's total experience. Buber says that in an I-thou relationship there is no agenda, no exploiting or using of the other, no relating merely to one segment of his person. One example of lack of presence is found in a type of interaction that frequently occurs between physician and patient. A highly competent and skillful physician may deal with the patient as if he were only a body.

---

[4] Martin Buber, *I and Thou*, New York: Scribner's, 1958.

[5] For a study that finds most middle-class marriages utilitarian, see John F. Cuber and Peggy Harroff, *The Significant Americans*, New York: Appleton-Century-Crofts, 1965. His description of what he calls utilitarian and intrinsic relationships has some similarity to the I-it, I-thou distinction.

At times such a specialized relationship may be necessary, a matter of life or death. Nevertheless, it is an I-it relationship.

I feel that Buber's conception of I-it and I-thou relationships is a vital glimpse into what exists, and what is possible, in human affairs. On the one hand, it is akin to the concepts of denial and labeling that I have been discussing; on the other hand, it is closely related to other important aspects of sociological and psychological theory. I will first discuss I-thouness and denial.

The attitude of I-thou encompasses, in part, the attitude of denial. The individual is accepted for what he is without judgment, comparison, evaluation, or criticism. Being present for the other means to experience the other as a whole, which means being conscious of the situation in which the other finds himself. Situational explanations of the other's behavior, which do not blame or criticize and which are part of the attitude of denial, are certainly subsumed by I-thou.

Similarly, the attitude of labeling is encompassed by the attitude of I-it. Seeing a deviant's behavior as determined by bad habits, criminal intent, neurotic character, or a mental disease is reducing him to an abstraction rather than seeing him in his full complexity. I am suggesting that the process of labeling the deviant is just one particular kind of manifestation of a much more general process characteristic of modern society—the generation of I-it relationships such as occur in contact with outsiders (strangers, enemies, and deviants), within bureaucracies, in utilitarian personal relationships, and, in fact, in most human contact in our society.

This is not to say that all forms of denial are I-thou. Denial may take the form of complete and supportive acceptance of the person, but it can also take the form of indifference, apathy, and so forth—kinds of behavior that have nothing in common with I-thou.

The attitude of denial may be a particular manifestation of the much more general attitude of I-thou, sometimes found in relationships between parents and children, teachers and students, friends and lovers. The attitude of denial is represented by the religious maxim, "Love the sinner but hate the sin." The attitude of labeling might be expressed by modifying the maxim to "Hate the sinner and the sin." Denial is typical of the informal handling of deviance that takes place among intimates in cohesive groups, and labeling is characteristic of the formal handling of deviance committed by persons either already outside the group or who are to be pushed out of the group.

It seems reasonable to assume, as Buber does, that the degree of categorization of persons is a fundamental .characteristic of an entire society in a given historical epoch. Buber argues, as Marx did, that life in modern urban, industrial societies is characterized by alienation at all levels—societal, interpersonal, and individual. At the societal level, the predominant form of organization is bureaucracy. At the interpersonal level, the predominant form of relationship is I-it. And at the level of the individual, the predominant type of person is the alienated man—detached from his institutions and culture, remote from others and even from himself—exemplified by a Kafka or Camus hero.

At the opposite pole are those historical or utopian societies that are represented as not reducing persons to categories. At the societal level, the predominant form of organization would be communal; at the interpersonal level, I-thou; and at the level of the individual, the unalienated individual, passionately engaged, and in intimate contact with at least one other person and with himself.

This is not to suggest that all modern societies are inevitably I-it, or that all preliterate societies are I-thou. Descriptions of preliterate societies indicate that they are incredibly diverse; some are as repressive and constricting as any modern society.[6]

THE SOCIALIZATION OF FEELING

On the basis of the extended discussions of categorization of persons by Marx, Weber, Buber, and the other authors referred to above, it seems that the organizing principles of a society based upon I-it relationships are hierarchy, predictability, and control, and for a society based upon I-thou relationships, equality, spontaneity, and freedom. The society based upon I-it relationships is symbolized by the assembly line, the clock and calendar, and the budget—lifeless apparatus to which human beings are yoked like beasts of burden. The ideal person for such servitude is one who is reliably obedient, predictable, and orderly. The society based upon I-thou relationships is symbolized by reverence for life, human relationships, and play. The ideal person for such a society is one who is loving, sensitive, and inquisitive.

For the organizing principles of a society to become stable and all-pervasive, rather than merely occasional, they must be built into the personalities of the members of the society by means of the socialization practices that the society employs with its children. Societies that stress hierarchy, order, and predictability must produce families that stress these same principles. Children in such societies are trained to obey commands by superiors in pursuit of fixed goals rather than to negotiate with equals in response to changing conditions.

With children, the only universal source of resistance to the parents' insistence on hierarchy, order, and control is the child's feelings. In families based upon I-it relationships, we might expect, therefore, that the

---

[6] A widely known statement of this fact can be found in Ruth Benedict, *Patterns of Culture*, Boston: Houghton Mifflin, 1934.

issue of how and when the child expresses his feelings would become the main battleground between child and parents. In particular, we would look for early and fundamental conflict over the two earliest, most frequent, and most insistent expressions of feeling by the child: his crying and screaming—that is, his expressions of grief and anger. Other feelings that should give rise to conflict over control are fear, laughter, and boredom, and feelings related to body functions such as elimination and sex. Although all of these feelings give rise to parent-child conflict, crying and screaming would seem to be the basic ones; none of the other expressions of feeling by the child begin as early as, or have the imperativeness of, crying and screaming.

In his discussion of the origins of repression, Freud clearly and emphatically pointed to the conflict between the parent's desire for control and the child's "biological" impulses. However, it seems to me that in emphasizing the repression of sexuality he made a fundamental error. Although it is true that the parents in an I-it relationship have moral compulsions about the child's sexuality, these concerns do not have the pressing immediacy that the child's crying has. Infants may take five or six months to even find their genitals, and fifteen or sixteen years to use them in a way that the parents would find publicly compromising. Other impulses also occasion moral concern in the parents, and, as in the case of elimination, present more immediate housekeeping considerations as well. But even with elimination, there is cultural buffering that prevents immediate, open conflict. In preliterate societies, parental attitudes about elimination allow the infant considerable leeway. Parental attitudes are quite different in modern urban societies, but diapers, rubber pants, and diaper services buffer the conflict. Even under the strictest circumstances, there is a grace period of a year or two before parental control is firmly exercised.

But with crying and screaming there are no buffers. From the instant of birth, the infant makes known his feelings directly and compellingly. The cry and the scream make the parents' sleep problematic. Emotionally, the child has the power to continually distract the attention of the parent and to awaken feelings of guilt as to whether the parent is fulfilling his or her obligations to the infant. The parents must find some way of dealing with crying and screaming, and they must find it immediately. It seems to me that the basic contours of the parent-child relationship and, therefore (as we will see below), of the child's personality, will be shaped by the tactics that the parents use to socialize the child's cry.

The emphasis I am placing on parental reaction to crying and screaming is not intended to suggest that the socialization of the other feelings, such as fear and sex, is unimportant. I am saying only that because the issue of control of the cry comes first, it usually establishes or manifests the basic orientation of parent to child. If this is the case, the socialization of the other feelings is very likely to follow the same pattern as the socialization of crying.

In a society based upon I-it relationships, the socialization of crying is carried out not only by parents but by persons in most other relationships besides the family—by friends, lovers, and other peers. In their study of the culture of childhood, the Opies report an extremely large list of derogatory terms for crying, as well as a large number of jeers and taunts, that are used by children. For example, the boys in one locality had twenty different names for a crybaby: "baby bunting, blubber, boo-baby, diddums, grizzle-guts, howler, leaky, Lumleyite (after a local boy), moaner, mother's little darling, sissy, slobber-baby, sniveler, softy, tap, Tearful Tilly, water-can, water-hog, waterworks, and weeping willow." A crying child may be told: "Go back to your bottle," "Don't make it wet on a dry day," "Mammy have to rock you to sleep," "He's got water on the brain," "He's turned on the tap," "Don't worry, he's just left his napkins (diapers)," and "He's just fallen out of his cot." [7] The socialization of crying is thus not just an idiosyncratic response of particular parents (although there is variation among parents in the severity of their punitiveness), but is part of a social institution that permeates the entire society.

Perhaps it is for this reason that in his treatment of socialization of emotions, the psychologist Tomkins gives principal attention to the socialization of crying. (The phrase that Tomkins uses is the socialization of "anguish-distress.")[8] According to Tomkins, the parents' pattern of reacting to the child's crying probably has enormous consequences for the child's adult personality. He contrasts two main patterns, which he calls the punitive and the reward socialization of crying.[9] In punitive socialization, the parent "punishes and tries to suppress the crying of the child"; in reward socialization, the parent "tries to reduce the crying of the child by removing the source and also by further rewarding the child with sympathy, to soothe the child."

These two socialization tactics, it seems to me, correspond in some ways to the distinction between I-it and I-thou relationships applied to child rearing. In punitive socialization, the adult is not present for—that is, he does not acknowledge, and has no interest in—the child's unique inner experience—his anguish or other distress. The parent wants external

[7] Iona Opie and Peter Opie, *The Lore and Language of Schoolchildren*, Oxford, London: 1959, pp. 186–88.

[8] Silvan S. Tomkins, "Distress-Anguish Dynamics: The Adult Consequences of the Socialization of Crying," Chapter 15 of *Affect, Imagery, Consciousness*, Vol. 2, New York: Springer, 1963, pp. 47–118.

[9] Similar distinctions, such as child-oriented versus thing-oriented socialization, are common in the literature on socialization. For a review cf. Robert R. Sears, Eleanor E. Maccoby, and Harry Levin, *Patterns of Child Rearing*, Evanston, Ill.: Row, Peterson, 1957.

compliance, obedience, and order, and punishes the child through physical means, such as the use of force and beating, or emotional means, such as terror, shame, contempt, or disgust.[10] In reward socialization, the parent attempts to be present for the child by acknowledging and accepting his anguish or other distress and by offering sympathy.

The correspondence is not exact, however. Though punitive socialization is clearly a case of an I-it relationship, reward socialization is not necessarily an indication of an I-thou relationship. A mechanical kind of rewarding process—in which the parent automatically and routinely rewards and sympathizes with the child in distress, without really being present—bears only a superficial resemblance to an I-thou relationship. In this context Tomkins speaks of sedation strategies (calming, quieting) in the socialization of crying, as an alternative to punishment.[11] Sedation, withdrawal, punishment, and even mechanical reward are all equally far from an I-thou relationship. The crucial element is not the gross external behavior of the parent but something more subtle: whether he is present for the child as a human being, trying to understand and respond to the child's unique experience.

Among the adult consequences of the punitive socialization of crying that Tomkins discusses, there are two that are of fundamental importance for the thesis presented here. The first consequence is usually an adult whose emotions are so severely repressed that he seems to others and even to himself to be virtually emotionless. Although the personality of this adult is well suited for human contact in which hierarchy, order, and predictability are emphasized, he is likely to be quite rigid in most areas and lacking in spontaneity and creativity. Like the bureaucracy he is apt to serve, he is suited for short-term efficiency in using means to an end, but is unlikely to be innovative, creative, or responsive to changing conditions.[12]

A second consequence of the punitive socialization of emotions is likely to be an individual who is as intolerant of emotions in others as his parents were of his own emotions as a child. As Tomkins points out, this intolerance has important social consequences in that it influences that individual's trust of and solidarity with others. The person whose emotions have been socialized punitively has learned to hide his most intense and deep-seated concerns from others, lest revelation of them cause him further suffering. The person whose emotions have been socialized with rewards

---

[10] Tomkins, *op. cit.*, pp. 132–156, V.II.

[11] *Ibid.*, pp. 112–14.

[12] For a theory that describes very precisely the relationship between creativity and the discharge of emotional distress, see Harvey Jackins, *The Human Side of Human Beings*, Seattle, Rational Island Press, 1965. A similar but less precise theory is found in Arthur Koestler, *The Act of Creation*, New York, Dell, 1964, especially Chapter IV, "From Humor to Discovery," and Chapter XII, "The Logic of the Moist Eye."

learns that his distress need not isolate him from others. On the contrary, it can be the "occasion of deepest intimacy and affirmation of love and concern." [13] We would expect societies that use punitive socialization to have a brittle solidarity based upon fear or contingent considerations. In a society that uses reward socialization, in contrast, we would expect a resilient and tough solidarity based upon trust and mutual concern.

PERSONALITY CHANGE AND SOCIAL CONTEXT

Persons whose emotions are repressed, interacting with other persons with similar personality structures, help further contain expression of emotions in a self-sustaining process. Such interaction is produced by, and produces, alienated relationships and institutions in a way that perpetuates itself continuously.

This is not to suggest, however, that once emotional repression occurs in a child, he is doomed to go through life as an alienated adult. Various circumstances in his life, such as contacts that lead to I-thou relationships, may result in substantial change in his personality and, therefore, in de-alienation. Another possibility for change is represented by psychotherapy, particularly a therapy oriented toward the release of repressed emotions.

In the psychotherapeutic method that Freud used early in his career, he found that one type of successful outcome was based upon what he called the "abreaction of arrears." [14] In these cases, patients discharged emotional distress such as fear, grief, and anger over long-forgotten earlier events in a way that seemed to lead to recovery. A more recent study by Symonds also supports this thesis.[15] Symonds sought published reports on successful psychotherapy that was traceable to events that occurred during the therapeutic session. Of the 68 cases he found, the successful outcomes were traceable to abreaction in 59, the great majority of cases. Similar results through catharsis of emotion are reported, though generally not documented, by Janov and other therapists.[16]

It appears, however, that personality change occurring in individuals in psychotherapy, who after all are dispersed in a society at large, is often not sufficient to interrupt the self-sustaining system of alienated relationships

[13] Tomkins, op. cit., p. 106.

[14] S. Freud and J. Breuer, Studies on Hysteria, New York: Basic Books, 1957, p. 285.

[15] Percival M. Symonds, "A Comprehensive Theory of Psychotherapy," American Journal of Orthopsychiatry (1954), 697–712.

[16] Arthur Janov, The Primal Scream, New York: Dell, 1970. A recent study does document the claim that abreaction reduces tension: Werner Karle et al., "Psychophysiological Changes in Abreactive Therapy—Study I: Primal Therapy," Psychotherapy: Theory, Research, and Practice, 10 (Summer, 1973), 117–22.

of which these persons are a part. Even with a skillful psychotherapy that effectively releases repressed emotion, the individual must eventually return, unaided, to cope with the same interpersonal social setting in which his difficulties arose in the first place. In many cases, after successful psychotherapy over a period of several years, the individual is unable to maintain his therapeutic gains. The pretherapy personality, no matter how successful the therapy, is not erased completely. After leaving therapy, and as distress from daily living accumulates, contacts with the unchanged interpersonal social structure revive the old personality, and it begins to lock itself in with that structure, as it did before therapy. In these cases the individual is back where he started from, even though he received excellent therapy. Much psychotherapy is not excellent: skill and attention are expensive and in short supply, and therapeutic gains are small. In such cases, gains are quickly lost when the patients are dispersed in the society.

What seems to be needed are ways of creating change that deal with individuals in social settings rather than in isolation. The key ingredient for such a procedure appears to be communication that allows for emotional release, on the one hand, and for the creation of a group in which there is strong social solidarity and which will help sustain the changes, on the other. As Tomkins suggests, the most effective procedure is probably one that combines these two elements, emotional discharge and social solidarity, for each leads to the other. The more open emotional discharge, the more solidarity, and vice versa. In the discussion below, I will cite several historical instances of procedures that seem to meet these requirements.

The first example that might be cited is Greek tragedy during the classical era of democracy in Athens. Aristotle suggested that the purpose of tragedy was to purge the members of the audience of pity and terror. Apparently, performances were occasions for the expression of crying and wailing. Speaking of Aristotle's reference to catharsis as the purging of pity, Lucas comments:

Since pity, especially in tragedy, is often pity for the dead or the bereaved, it is [also] akin to the shared or public lamentation which is part of life in small and closely knit communities. [There is a suggestion] that the audience luxuriated in community sorrow, "surrendering itself" to lamentation and taking part in mourning along with actors and chorus.[17]

A second type of social form that meets individual needs in a social setting can be found in certain religious sects such as the Shakers and the Quakers (shaking is a form that the discharge of fear takes) and, more recently, in black churches in the United States and in white fundamen-

---

[17] D. W. Lucas, "Pity, Fear, and Katharsis," Appendix II in his edition of Aristotle's *Poetics*, Oxford: Clarendon Press, 1968, p. 273.

talist groups such as the Church of God in Christ (the "Holy Rollers"). Group meetings in these sects stimulate collective catharsis in such a way that the needs of individuals to release tension or distressful emotion are met. At the same time, this collective catharsis gives rise to heightened solidarity and a sense of cultural community within the group. As long as this form leads to genuine and spontaneous emotional release, it serves a vital need for the members and develops an extremely cohesive group.

A third instance is found in the history of the Chinese Communist revolution, in which several social forms that led to catharsis were used. One form was called "Speak Bitterness" meetings. Jack Belden, who witnessed such meetings, describes them in this way:

People confessed, not their sins, but their sorrows. This had the effect of creating emotional solidarity. For when people poured out their sorrows to each other, they realized they were all together on the same sad voyage through life, and from recognition of this they drew closer to one another, achieved common sentiments, took sustenance and hope.[18]

Another form used by the Chinese Communists was the theater. Dramatic scenes depicting the oppression of the old society caused mass weeping:

As the tragedy of [a] poor peasant's family unfolded, the women around me wept openly and unashamedly. On every side as I turned to look tears were coursing down their faces. No one sobbed, no one cried out but all wept together in silence. The agony on the stage seemed to have unlocked a thousand painful memories, a bottomless reservoir of suffering that no one could control . . . the women, huddled one against the other in their dark padded jackets, shuddered as if stirred by a gust of wind . . . abruptly the music stopped, the silence on the stage was broken only by the chirping of a cricket. At that moment I become aware of a new quality in the reaction of the audience. Men were weeping, and I along with them.[19]

In some ways, these social forms are related to primitive religious ceremonies. One such ceremony is the exorcism of demons. The anthropologist Obeyesekere reports an exorcism that occurred in a Ceylonese tribe.[20] A woman was said by her husband to be delusional, mute, and withdrawn. The priest assembled all of her relatives for an exorcism ceremony. He spoke to the woman, calling upon the god Vishnu to speak through her. The woman replied in a deep voice to his questions. The priest's questions and her answers pointed to various conflicts that existed in her interpersonal environment. The priest's adroit questions brought the conflicts into the open. The emotional release that occurred and the rebuilding of the network of understanding between the woman and her relatives resulted in a "cure."

[18] Jack Belden, *China Shakes the World*, New York: Monthly Review Press, 1949, pp. 487–88.
[19] William Hinton, *Fanshen*, New York: Vintage, 1966, pp. 314–15.
[20] Gananath Obeyesekere, "The Idiom of Demonic Possession: A Case Study," *Social Science and Medicine*, 4 (1970), 97–111. Reprinted in this volume, pp. 134–151.

The American psychiatrist Ross Speck has developed a means of treating "mental illness" that is based upon similar social and psychological concepts.[21] Speck believes that what is conventionally called "mental illness" represents a breakdown of the natural social network of which the patient is a member. His therapy, therefore, is for the network as well as the patient. His treatment is an attempt to reconstruct the network. Like the Ceylonese priest, he first assembles the network of relatives, friends, and neighbors; he then seeks to reopen communication among its members and to clarify the misunderstanding and conflicts that exist between the patient and the other members of the network.

A final instance of a social form that meets individual needs in a social setting is the current Chinese Communist procedure for treating "mental illness." The treatment rests largely upon group discussion in which there is an attempt to reintegrate the patient into his society.[22] The techniques used lay heavy emphasis on political analysis. Using the thought of Mao Tse-tung, each patient is given an opportunity to stand before the group and voice the oppression to which he has been exposed, analyzing his class background and criticizing his own performance. These procedures seem to meet both individual and collective needs: the patient learns to acknowledge his own behavior rather than to disassociate it, and he learns to explain it on the basis of the political ideology that is common to the members of the group. Like the "Speak Bitterness" meetings, such analysis often results in catharsis.

According to George Hatem, a high official in the Chinese Ministry of Health, similar procedures were used in a highly successful rehabilitation of prostitutes:

At so-called "Speak Bitterness" meetings, the girls were encouraged to rid themselves of shame and hostility by recounting their pasts and their oppression. They were given hours of catharsis.[23]

All of the above examples have two elements in common: first, individuals are allowed the opportunity to release repressed emotion, and, second, individual needs are dealt with in the context of an interpersonal social network rather than in a setting isolated from this network.[24] Under these conditions, substantial changes in the personalities of individuals are possible through emotional discharge, and these changes have a good chance of long-term stability. The network in which change takes place

[21] Ross Speck and Carolyn L. Attneave, "Social Network Intervention," in Jay Haley, (ed.), *Changing Families,* New York: Grune and Stratton, 1971.

[22] Ruth and Victor Sidel, "The Human Services in China," *Social Policy* (March-April, 1972), 25–33.

[23] Quoted by Lloyd Shearer, "Dr. George Hatem—The Most Famous American in China," *Parade* (August 12, 1973), 4–5.

[24] For a contemporary method that combines these two elements, see my article "Re-evaluation Counseling: Social Implications," *Journal of Humanistic Psychology,* 12 (1972), 58–71.

becomes a supportive enclave in which the change can be maintained. The individual is not cast adrift on his own. In addition, the network may become the social base for institutional change, as was the case with the Chinese Communist groups. Thus, such networks can function as "transitional communities" that protect individual change, and they may become the base for change in the larger society.

SUMMARY

In this chapter, I have attempted to integrate labeling theory with other sociological and psychological theory. I have defined the labeling-denial continuum in terms of the degree of categorization of persons as *only* deviants. This definition allows the concept of labeling to be subsumed under a very general phenomenon, the categorization of persons, which proceeds apace in the entire social structure, such as in bureaucratized relationships that occur in industry and education, and in alienated interpersonal relationships. Thus, labeling can be seen as a particular manifestation, in the area of deviance, of a pervasive process that occurs in most other areas of human contact in modern societies.

Because this definition of labeling relates it to many vital social and psychological processes, we are led to look for the roots of labeling—and means for its reduction, or at least the reduction of some of its consequences—in sociological and psychological points of view. I have argued that if the organizing principles of modern societies are hierarchy, predictability, and control, we would expect that the crucial molding of the character of individuals in contemporary societies would occur in the socialization of feeling, particularly the socialization of crying and screaming.

I have argued that repression of emotions is produced by, and produces, rigidity, authoritarianism, and brutality in a reciprocally enhancing, virtually self-sustaining process. Conversely, I have argued that release of repressed emotion produces, and is produced by, spontaneity, mutual trust, and solidarity, and that such processes may lead to substantial personality change. It seems crucial, however, that occasions for emotional release be social; otherwise, the changes occurring among dispersed individuals and the solidarity that is a product of emotional release in social settings may dissipate. I cited several examples of procedures that have led to emotional release in social settings—Greek tragedy, religious revivalism, the Chinese Communist group meetings, demon exorcism in Ceylon, and network therapy in a large American city. These examples point to the need for current therapeutic or dramatic forms, or other ceremonies yet to be discovered, which would deal with individual and collective needs simultaneously.

REFERENCES

Belden, Jack, *China Shakes the World*. New York: Monthly Review Press, 1949.

Benedict, Ruth, *Patterns of Culture*. Boston: Houghton Mifflin, 1934.

Berger, Peter, and Pullberg, Stanley, "Reification and the Sociological Critique of Consciousness," *History and Theory*, 4, no. 2 (1965), 196–211.

Buber, Martin, *I and Thou*. New York: Scribner's, 1958.

Freud, Sigmund, and Joseph Breuer, *Studies on Hysteria*. New York: Basic Books, 1957.

Garfinkel, Harold, "Conditions for Successful Degradation Ceremonies," *American Journal of Sociology*, 61 (1956), 420–24.

Hinton, William, *Fanshen*. New York: Vintage, 1966.

Jackins, Harvey, *The Human Side of Human Beings*. Seattle: Rational Island Press, 1965.

Janov, Arthur, *The Primal Scream*. New York: Dell, 1970.

Karle, Werner, et al., "Psychophysiological Changes in Abreactive Therapy—Study I: Primal Therapy," *Psychotherapy: Theory, Research and Practice*, 10 (Summer, 1973), 117–22.

Koestler, Arthur, *The Act of Creation*. New York: Dell, 1964.

Linsky, Arnold S., "Community Homogeneity and Exclusion of the Mentally Ill: Rejection Versus Consensus about Deviance," *Journal of Health and Social Behavior*, 11 (1970), 304–11.

Lucas, D. W., "Pity, Fear, and Katharsis," Appendix II in his edition of Aristotle's *Poetics*. Oxford: Clarendon Press, 1968.

Obeyesekere, Gananath, "The Idiom of Demonic Possession: A Case Study," *Social Science and Medicine*, 4 (1970), 97–111.

Opie, Iona, and Opie, Peter, *The Lore and Language of Schoolchildren*. Oxford; London, 1959.

Scheff, Thomas J., "Users and Non-users of a Student Psychiatric Clinic," *Journal of Health and Human Behavior*, 7 (1966), 114–21.

————, "Re-evaluation Counseling: Social Implications," *Journal of Humanistic Psychology*, 12 (1972), 58–71.

Sears, Robert R., Eleanor E. Maccoby, and Harry Levin, *Patterns of Child Rearing*, Evanston, Ill.: Row, Peterson, 1957.

Sidel, Ruth, and Victor Sidel, "The Human Services in China," *Social Policy* (March-April, 1972), 25–33.

Shearer, Lloyd, "Dr. George Hatem—The Most Famous American in China," *Parade* (August 13, 1973), 4–5.

Speck, Ross, "Psychotherapy of the Social Network of a Schizophrenic Family," *Family Process*, 6 (1967), 208–14.

Symonds, Percival M., "A Comprehensive Theory of Psychotherapy," *American Journal of Orthopsychiatry*, 24 (1954), 697–712.

Tomkins, Silvan S., *Affect-Imagery-Consciousness*. New York: Springer, 1963.

8

PARANOIA OR PERSECUTION:
THE CASE OF SCHREBER
Morton Schatzman

In the article that follows, Schatzman, an American psychiatrist, brilliantly re-examines the Schreber case, a bizarre story that links the madness of a 19th century German judge with the child-rearing practices of his father, an eminent educator. The article can be used to illustrate several themes that are of central importance in this volume.

First, surely the case demonstrates the ambiguous status of received ideas of insanity, a theme that is implicit in the discussion of labeling theory in Part I of this book. By conventional definition, certainly Judge Schreber was mad. He thought that he was being persecuted by God, by "little devils." He did not realize that he was suffering, not from current persecution, but from reminiscences. He did not have sufficient insight to connect his distress with the way in which his father oppressed him as a child. Yet in another sense, he was much saner than most of the other people of his era. His memoirs identify as oppression and torture what his contemporaries, including Freud, accepted as normal child-rearing practices. (As Schatzman indicates in the article below, Freud actually praised the father's child rearing practices: ". . . His activities in favour of promoting the harmonious upbringing of the young . . ." [1]) His reminiscences have helped bring to light the incredible orientation of his father toward children. What is called madness may, as in this case, mean steadfast opposition to the particular kind of oppression that is held in esteem by current social standards. As labeling theory suggests, there is an element of arbitrariness and blindness in most social definitions of deviance.

The second point that we can make from the Schreber case is that a wider conceptualization of labeling is possible, which includes both social and psychological aspects and which does not sacrifice the iconoclastic thrust of labeling theory. The usual direction of the societal reaction to deviance is to seek a psychological explanation for deviance, which places the responsibility within the deviant, and to provide a situational explanation for conforming individuals ("It could have happened to anyone"). The Schreber case suggests that it may be profitable to look at both situational and psychological explanations, but to reverse the direction of the pristine form of the societal reaction. Given the extravagant brutality of the way that Judge Schreber, the "deviant," was raised, such an explanation would recognize the source of his suffering. We explain his "delusions" less in terms of his personality than in terms of the circumstances under which he was

Reprinted from *Family Process*, 10 (1971) 177–207. See also his book *Soul Murder: Persecution in the Family*, Random House: New York, 1973.

[1] Cited in the article below, p. 104.

raised as a child. The main puzzle does not lie with Judge Schreber but with his father. We are directed to look for a psychological explanation of the father's behavior, even though it conformed to the standards of his era. In King Lear, *Lear asks, "Is there anything in nature which makes such hard hearts?" How can we explain the extraordinary behavior of the elder Schreber?*

Tomkins's analysis of the socialization of distress suggests that fellow feeling and sympathy toward others is crucially dependent on the way in which one's distress has been socialized. Persons who are punished, ignored, or rejected when they are distressed will learn to not accept or even acknowledge distress in themselves or in others. The repression of feeling leads to an emphasis on order and control rather than on sympathy and spontaneity.

This analysis has many elements in common with a study by Wilhelm Reich.[2] *Reich argues that emotional and sexual repression was the key element in the brutal authoritarianism of the German family, and of the German state. From the point of view of Tomkins's theory, however, Reich, like Freud, greatly overemphasized the significance of specifically sexual repression. The area of sexual behavior, it seems, is simply one of many specific behavioral areas of conflict between the child's feelings and the parents' insistence upon control. Conflict between parent and child in all of these areas—such as sex, eating, sleeping, and elimination—are very early arenas for emotional repression. Even though Reich overemphasized sexual repression in his theory, he dealt exclusively with emotional repression in his actual practice of psychotherapy. Reich's psychotherapy was oriented solely to the discharge of repressed emotions, with emphasis on crying and screaming.*[3]

According to Tomkins's theory, complete suppression of distress produces an individual who will be absolutely intolerant of distress in others. We are led, therefore, to explain the elder Schreber's systematic brutality toward children in terms of his character. We can understand his character in turn, by looking to the large social network of German parents whose own characters were developed in repressive authoritarian families.

The systematized inhumanity of the senior Schreber's methods of childrearing represent punitive socialization at its most extreme. These extreme methods apparently had devastating consequences for his children. Of his two children whose fates are known, one, Judge Schreber, became mad, and the other, also a male, was a suicide. Less extreme and complete methods of punitive socialization should lead to less extreme, but still consequential adult outcomes. We might expect that the rigid orientation toward the treatment of infants in American families in the 1930's and '40's, characterized by feeding schedules, would not usually produce adults who are suicidal or "delusional" but, nevertheless, whose emotions are repressed.[4] *Such a middle level of emotional repression might give rise to adults who are "out of touch" with their feelings. This condition, as R. D. Laing has suggested, is so prevalent in modern societies that it constitutes "normal alienation from experience."*[5]

Finally, a close reading of this article provides evidence supporting the central point of Part II, that it is the specific repression of emotion, through punitive socialization of crying, screaming, and so on, which produces madness. The central importance of suppressing the child's expressions of emotional distress, using both physical and emotional coercion, is clearly stated by the elder Schreber:

---

[2] Wilhelm Reich, *The Mass Psychology of Facism,* Farrar, Straus & Giroux: New York, 1965.

[3] For a discussion of Reichian therapy by a patient, see Orson Bean, *Me and the Orgone,* New York: St. Martin's, 1971.

[4] For a discussion of historical change in child rearing, see C. B. Stendler, "Sixty Years of Child Training Practices," *Journal of Pediatrics,* 36 (1950) 122-34.

[5] R. D. Laing, *The Politics of Experience,* Ballantine, New York, 1967, 25-30.

One must look at the moods of the little ones which are announced by screaming without reason and crying . . . If one has convinced oneself that no real need, no disturbing or painful condition, no sickness is present, one can be assured that the screaming is only and simply the expression of a mood, a whim, the first appearance of self-will. . . . One has to step forward in a positive manner: by quick distraction of the attention, stern words, threatening gestures, rapping against the bed . . . or when all of this is of no avail—by moderate, intermittent, bodily admonishments consistently repeated until the child calms down or falls asleep. . . .

Such a procedure is necessary only once or at most twice and one is master *of the child forever. From now on a glance, a word, a single threatening gesture is sufficient to rule the child.*[6]

The elder Schreber explicitly cautions the parent against the procedure that Tomkins calls *reward socialization.*

If the child is lifted from the bed and carried around each time he makes noise—without checking if there is really something wrong—and is calmed by gentleness of one kind or another, this may often lead to the appearance of the emotion of spite later in the life of the child. I wish mothers and nursemaids would recognize the importance of this point![7]

It appears that the elder Schreber's program of extreme punitive socialization of the emotions of his children led them to suicide and madness.

In summary, Schatzman's analysis of the Schreber case can be used to illustrate three points. First, that our conventional ideas of insanity are often arbitrary, and, in this case, utterly blind, a position that is congruent with the labeling theory of mental illness. Secondly, that labeling theory can be broadened by combining it with analysis at the level of individual psychology, but reversing the usual stance; that is, by using situational analysis to understand the behavior of the labeled deviant, and character analysis for the understanding of the behavior of the labelers. Finally, the article contributes evidence supporting Tomkin's insistence on the fundamental importance of the socialization of emotions. The younger Schreber's irrational behavior may have had its source in his father's rigid child-rearing practices, which was a program for the systematic respression of emotion.

Psychoanalysts have built their theories about persons called paranoid upon data gathered mostly from the persons themselves. What they know of the childhood and family life of their patients is derived mainly from what their patients tell them. Since patients, like everyone else, never report entirely or precisely what they experience, this information is always incomplete and can be misleading.

Freud's (5) analysis of Daniel Paul Schreber is unique among his case studies in that a source of "raw" data about Schreber's childhood, which Freud did not use, still exists. Schreber's father, a physician, orthopedist, and pedagogue, wrote eighteen books and booklets, many of which are about his methods of educating children; he applied them to his own children. Although Freud knew of Schreber's father, he ignored his

---

[6] See p. 106, below.
[7] See p. 106, below.

writings as data—as did those who wrote about Schreber for the next fifty years—even though the father's books had been widely read and are still available. Freud's analysis of Schreber is a pivotal statement of the psychoanalytic theory of psychosis and has had much influence. It is the origin of the view, held by most psychoanalysts, that paranoia arises as a "defense" against homosexual love, that is, that the paranoid person is persecuted by his (or her) unconscious love, specifically for his (or her) parent of the same sex, which he (or she) experiences consciously as persecution from outside.

Schreber is considered a classic case of paranoia and schizophrenia. Eugen Bleuler (3), who invented the term schizophrenia and developed the concept, thought Schreber was paranoid, schizophrenic, hallucinated, deluded, dissociated, autistic, and ambivalent. He never mentions Schreber's father.

Twelve years ago William Niederland (15), an American psychoanalyst, pointed out some striking likenesses between some of Schreber's odd thoughts and his father's techniques of bringing up children. (I use several of Niederland's examples in what follows.)

I have read some of the father's writings and have found that several of Schreber's peculiar experiences for which he was labeled paranoid, schizophrenic, insane, and so forth, can be linked to specific procedures of his father; that the father's child-rearing practices could confuse any child; and that he would have forbidden a child to see how confusing his methods are.

I wish to relate the son's strange experiences to the child-rearing practices of his father. In terms of set theory, consider Dr. Schreber's methods of rearing children as elements of a set F and his son's peculiar experiences as elements of a set S. If an experience of the son is an *image* of a procedure of his father, we can call that experience a *transformation* of his father's procedure. I wish to define the operations by which elements of F are *transformed* into elements of S.

Although I confine myself to the study of Schreber's mind and his father's behavior, my findings, and how I construe them, may help in the understanding of others seen as paranoid or schizophrenic.

What I have found brings other issues into view. Irony is everywhere. An eminent pedagogue has a psychotic son; it does not hurt his reputation. Freud, an avid reader, neglects books on child rearing—as do his followers—by a man whose son's childhood experiences he tries to derive. German parents rear their children by the ideas of a man whom many people now would see as sadistic or mentally ill.

SON

Schreber, the son (1842–1911), was a German judge. He began a career as a mental patient at forty-two, spent thirteen of his next twenty-seven years in mental asylums, and died there. At sixty-one he published *Memoirs of My Nervous Illness* (19), a book he compiled from notes about his experiences and thoughts while "suffering from a nervous illness." Although he started the work in a mental asylum with no idea of publishing, he changed his mind as he progressed with it. He came to think that "observations of my personal fate during my lifetime would be of value both for science and the knowledge of religious truth." The *Memoirs* is the source of Freud's data about Schreber; Freud and Schreber never met.   •

For many years during his "nervous illness," Schreber endured painful and humiliating bodily experiences. He thought they were "miracles" (*Wunder*) that God performed, through "rays," upon his body. These experiences, and especially his view of their origin, led others to consider him crazy. Here he discusses them:

From the first beginnings of my contact with God up to the present day my body has continuously been the object of divine miracles. If I wanted to describe all these miracles in detail I could fill a whole book with them alone. I may say that hardly a single limb or organ in my body escaped being temporarily damaged by miracles, nor a single muscle being pulled by miracles, either moving or paralyzing it according to the respective purpose.

Even now the miracles which I experience hourly are still of a nature to frighten every other human being to death; only by getting used to them through the years have I been able to disregard most of what happens as trivialities. But in the first year of my stay at Sonnenstein (the mental asylum) the miracles were of such a threatening nature that I thought I had to fear almost incessantly for my life, my health or my reason. (19, p. 131)

This, as indeed the whole report about the miracles enacted on my body, will naturally sound extremely strange to all other human beings, and one may be inclined to see in it only the product of a pathologically vivid imagination. In reply I can only give the assurance that hardly any memory from my life is more certain than the miracles recounted in this chapter. What can be more definite for a human being than what he has lived through and felt on his own body?" (19, p. 132)

These experiences caused him great suffering and interfered with everything he did. Here are five "miracles" he describes; I follow each of them with passages from his father's books:

SON AND FATHER

SON:

Miracles of heat and cold were and still are daily enacted against me . . . always with the purpose of preventing the natural feelings of bodily well-being. . . . During the *cold-miracle* the blood is forced out of the extremities, so causing a subjective feeling of cold . . . during the *heat-miracle* the blood is forced towards my face and head in which of course coolness is the condition corresponding to a general sense of well-being. *From youth accustomed to enduring both heat and cold,* these miracles troubled me little . . . I myself have often been forced to seek heat and cold. (19, pp. 145–46) [Italics here and in all the passages I quote are my own except where specified otherwise.]

FATHER:

". . . starting about three months after birth *cleansing of the infant's skin should be by cold ablutions only,* . . . in order to physically toughen up the child." (21, p. 41)

He advises *warm baths for infants* up to six months. Then "one may pass to *cool and cold general ablutions* which should be performed at least once daily and for which the body should be prepared by prior *local applications of cold water*" (21, p. 40). He says *cold baths* are the accepted rule after four or five years old.

SON:

My *eyes* and the *muscles of the lids* which serve to open and close them were an almost uninterrupted target for miracles. The eyes were always of particular importance. . . . The miracles on my eyes were performed by "little men." . . . These "little men" were one of the most remarkable and even to me most mysterious phenomena. . . . These occupied with the opening and closing of the eyes stood above the eyes in the eyebrows and these pulled the eyelids up or down as they pleased with fine filaments like cobwebs. . . . Whenever I showed signs of being unwilling to allow my eyelids to be pulled up and down and actually opposed it, the "little men" became annoyed and expressed this by calling me "wretch"; if I wiped them off my eyes with a sponge, it was considered by the rays as a sort of crime against God's gift of miracles.

By the way wiping them away had only a very temporary effect, because the "little men" were each time set down afresh. (19, pp. 136–38)

As often as an insect . . . appears, a miracle simultaneously affects the *direction of my gaze.* I have not mentioned the miracle before, but it has been regularly practised for years. Rays after all continually *want to see what pleases them.* . . . My eye-muscles are therefore *influenced to move in a certain direction.* . . . (19, p. 186)

FATHER:

He insists on eye exercises for children in his booklet, *The Systematically Planned Sharpening of the Sense Organs* (24): to distract quickly a child's visual attention, to force him to estimate dimensions of similar objects at different distances, to judge various distances, etc. (p. 11). In another book (23), in a section called "The Care, Education and Sharpening of Sense Organs," he recommends "the proper alternation between looking near and far . . . one should get the children into the habit of recognizing the first traces of tiredness of the eyes or of that well-known slightly burning or irritating feeling of overstimulation: in this case especially, besides rest, spraying the eyes with cool water is recommended; *repeated visual exercises* looking over mildly lit green areas with sharp or precise fixing on distant, barely recognizable, objects, . . . just as important are exercises in close-up vision, like precise observation and comparison of small objects . . ." (p. 215).

He recommends that children's "eyelids, eyebrows, and temporal areas be treated daily with cold water," which he thinks will sharpen their vision. (Niederland [15, p. 387], quoted from D. G. M. Schreber [20])

SON:

He describes a painful experience he calls "the so-called coccyx miracle." "This was an extremely painful caries-like state of the lowest vertebrae. Its purpose was *to make sitting and even lying down impossible.* Altogether I was not allowed to remain for long in *one and the same position* or at the same occupation: when I was walking one attempted to force me to lie down, and when I was *lying down one wanted to chase me off* my bed. Rays did not seem to appreciate at all that a human being who actually exists must be somewhere. . . . I had become an embarrassing being for the rays (for God), in whatever position or circumstance I might be or whatever occupation I undertook" (19, p. 139).

FATHER:

He warns parents and educators to fight the child's tendency to sit unevenly because he says it harms the spinal column. ". . .One must see to it that children always sit straight and even-sided on both buttocks at once . . . leaning neither to the right or left side. . . . As soon as they start to lean back . . . or bend their backs, the time has come to exchange at least for a few minutes the seated position for the absolutely still, supine one. If this is not done . . . the backbones will be deformed . . ." (23, p. 100).

". . . *Half resting in lying or wallowing positions should not be allowed:* if children are awake they should be alert and hold themselves in straight, active positions and be busy; in general each thing which could lead towards laziness and softness (for example the sofa in the children's room) should be kept away from their circle of activity." (23, p. 150)

These procedures and the following ones were part of the father's program to keep the bodies of children of all ages straight at all times:

when they stood, sat, walked, played, lay down, or slept (see Figures 1 and 2). He thought children must sleep in a straight position only, flat on their backs; babies under four months must lie only on their backs when resting. It is important, he taught, to start with infants, for he thought it harder to train older children. In his book, *The Harmful Body Positions and Habits of Children, Including a Statement of Counteracting Measures* (22), he presented as medical fact his false idea that if a child lies too long on one side, his body on that side may be damaged, "the nutrition is impaired," the "flow of juices is impeded," the "blood stops and piles up in the vessels," and the vessels "lose a large part of their life tension" (p. 12). This may lead later to paralysis of the arm and foot on that side, he said (23, p. 54).

SON:

One of the most horrifying miracles was the so-called *compression-of the-chest-miracle* . . . ; it consisted in the *whole chest wall being compressed,* so that the state of oppression caused by the lack of breath was transmitted to my whole body. (19, p. 133)

FATHER:

He invented a device called *Schrebersche Geradhalter* (Schreber's straight-holder) to force children to sit straight (see Figures 3 and 4). This was an iron cross-bar fastened to the table at which the child sat to read or write. The bar pressed against the collar bones and the front of the shoulders to prevent forward movements or crooked posture. He says the child could not lean for long against the bar "because of the *pressure* of the hard object against the bones and the consequent *discomfort;* the child will return on his own to the straight position" (23, p. 204). "I had a Geradhalter manufactured which proved itself to be suitable after multiple tests *on my own children.* . . ." (p. 203) Besides the physical effects, he says it is also "an effective moral means" (p. 205). (He says that the vertical bar which supported it was "useful" too since it prevented young children from crossing their legs.)

He also tied a *belt* to the child's bed which ran across *the child's chest* to ensure that the child's body remained supine and straight when sleeping (see Figures 5 and 6).

SON:

This was perhaps the most abominable of all miracles—next to the compression-of-the-chest-miracle; the expression used for it if I remember correctly was "the head-compressing-machine" (Kopfzusammenschnürungsmachine: literally, the head-together-tying machine). . . . The "little devils" . . . *compressed my head as though in a vise* by turning a kind of screw, causing my head temporarily to assume an elongated almost pear-shaped form. It had an extremely threatening effect, particularly as it was accompanied by severe pain. The screws were loosened

FIGURES 1 THROUGH 8 ARE PHOTOSTATIC REPRODUCTIONS
FROM DR. SCHREBER'S *Kallipädie* (1858).

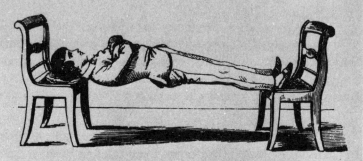

Figure 1 (p. 197) The "bridge." Dr. Schreber thought a forward slump of a child's head and shoulders when walking was "a clear expression of weakness, dumbness and cowardice." He devised the "bridge," an exercise "to strengthen the back and neck muscles" of children who slumped.

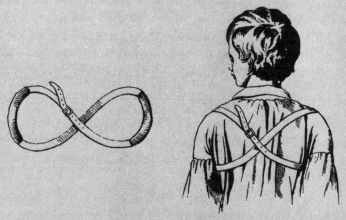

Figure 2 (p. 198) A shoulder band to prevent "falling forward of the shoulders." Dr. Schreber thought it should be worn every day, all day, until "the bad habit is regulated." The shaded parts of the band on the left are metal springs to rest on the front of the shoulders.

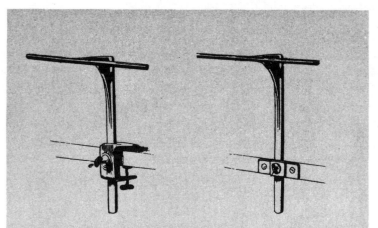

Figure 3 (p. 203) The Geradhalter. *On the left is a portable one for home use. The one on the right was fixed to desks at school.*

Figure 4 (p. 205) The Geradhalter *in use.*

temporarily but only very gradually, so that the *compressed state usually continued for some time.* (19, p. 138)

I suffer from almost uninterrupted headaches of a kind certainly unknown to other human beings and hardly comparable to ordinary headaches. They are *tearing* and *pulling* pains. (19, p. 201)

FATHER:

He invented a *Kopfhalter* (head-holder) to prevent the child's head from falling forward or sideways. The Kopfhalter was a strap clamped at one end to the child's hair and at the other to his underwear so that it *pulled* his hair if he did not hold his head straight (see Figure 7). It served as a "reminder" to keep the head straight: "The consciousness that the head cannot be lowered past a certain point soon becomes a habit." He admits it was apt to produce "*a certain stiffening effect* on the head" and should therefore be used only one or two hours a day (23, pp. 198–99).

He also had a chinband built which was held to the head by a helmet-like device (see Figure 8). This was to ensure proper growth of the jaw and teeth (23, pp. 219–20).

These comparisons show uncanny similarities. It is as if the father taught his son a language of sensory stimuli by which to experience parts of his own body.[1]

Niederland wonders if Schreber's experiences of having been tied and strapped by the father into orthopedic apparatus are the origin of the "divine miracles" of "being tied-to-earth" and "fastened-to-rays."[2]

God is inseparably tied to my person through my nerves' power of attraction which for some time past has been inescapable. There is no possibility of God freeing Himself from my nerves for the rest of my life. (19, p. 209)

The son thinks the "miracles" are enacted upon objective anatomical organs of his body. He does not see that he is *re*enacting his father's behavior toward his body.

Schreber suffers from reminiscences. His body embodies his past. He retains memories of what his father did to him as a child; although part of his mind knows they are memories, "he" does not. He is considered insane not only because of the quality of his experiences, but because he misconstrues their *mode;* he *remembers,* in some cases perfectly accurately, how his father treated him, but he thinks he *perceives* events occurring in the present of which he imagines God, rays, little men, and so on are the agents. He knows what he most needs to know, but does not know he knows it. When he calls his experiences "miracles," he denies what he

[1] In the idiom of Lacan, the French psychoanalyst, Schreber's "symptoms" would be "metaphors," that is, "terms" that "signify" orginal traumas. See Lacan (9).

[2] Niederland tries to show that his findings confirm Freud's conclusions about why Schreber became paranoid; he does not see that his findings call for radically new hypotheses.

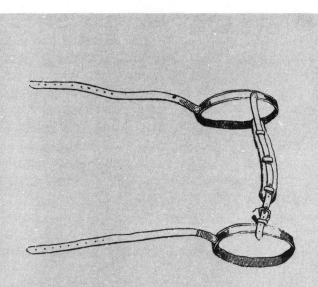

Figure 5 (p. 174) A belt for the sleeping child.

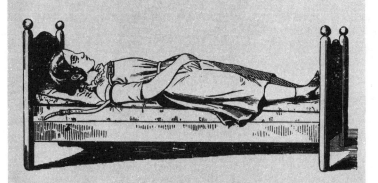

Figure 6 (174) The belt in use.

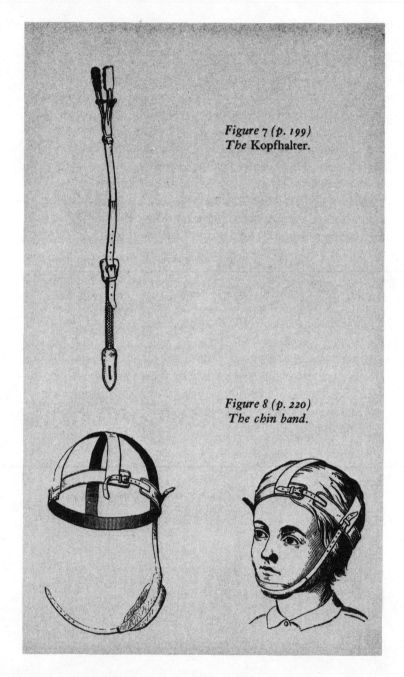

Figure 7 (p. 199)
The Kopfhalter.

Figure 8 (p. 220)
The chin band.

knows, denies he is denying anything, and denies there is anything to deny, *and* he denies those denials too.

Schreber's "forgetting" is not the usual amnesia for events of early childhood; his father used belts across the chests of sleeping children starting at seven or eight years old, and the *Geradhalter* and *Kopfhalter* with eight- to sixteen-year-olds.

It is as if Schreber is forbidden by a rule to see the role his father has played in his suffering, and is forbidden by another rule to see anything there is he does not see, and it is as if a rule forbids him to see that rule, or *that* a rule might exist. For instance, he never says he cannot find what his experiences mean, and that he cannot because a rule stops him, or that he cannot and does not know why he cannot. He is certain he knows what they mean; although he discusses their meaning in detail, he never connects them with his father.

The use of one's mind to try to understand the meaning of experiences that occur in one's mind can be uniquely problematic. Ashby (1) in *An Introduction to Cybernetics* said that when a man cannot see some of the variables of a system, the "system" represented by the remainder may develop remarkable, even *miraculous,* properties (p. 114). A mind that observes itself is both the observer and the system observed; the variables it cannot see may be those it does not *wish* to see, whether or not it knows of its wish. Experiences that arise from a region of one's mind of which one is not ordinarily conscious may appear to have extraordinary sources and qualities.

Why did Schreber turn memories into "miracles"? My hypothesis is that his father had forbidden him to see the truth about his past. His father had demanded that children love, honor, and obey their parents. As I illustrate later, he taught parents a method explicitly designed to force children not to feel bitterness or anger toward their parents, even when the feelings might be justified. He wished to rid children of such "dangerous" feelings. Schreber, in order to link his suffering with his father, would have had to consider his father's behavior toward him as "bad." This, I infer, his father had forbidden him to do. He is unable, or unwilling, to violate his father's view of what his view of his father should be. Prohibited from seeing the true origin of his torments, he calls them miracles. As a result, he is considered crazy.

He was not alone in failing to see the link. No one else did either, including the psychiatrists who treated him and those who wrote about him.

He could almost see it; he accuses his doctor, Flechsig:

"You, *like so many doctors,* could not completely resist the temptation of using a patient as an object for experimentation." (19, p. 34)

It would be important to know how and why Schreber *stopped* repressing and started reexperiencing sometime after forty the suffering of his childhood, albeit he did not know he was remembering it.

FATHER

The father was Dr. Daniel Gottlieb Moritz Schreber; he wrote books about human anatomy and physiology, hygiene and physical culture; he was interested in body building by gymnastics. He began the *Schreber Vereine*, associations for calisthenics, gardening, and fresh-air activities. He added moral principles to his precepts for physical health, joining them into a comprehensive educational system for parents and teachers. If his readers applied his ideas to their daily lives and their children's, he said, a stronger race of men would result. He dedicated his *Kallipädie* (23), from which I quote later, "to the welfare of future generations." The full title of the book is *Education Towards Beauty by Natural and Balanced Elevation of Normal Body Formation, of Life-Supporting Health, and of Mental Ennoblement, Especially by the Use, if Possible, of Special Educational Means: for Parents, Educators and Teachers.* He died at fifty-three when the author of the *Memoirs* was nineteen.

Freud (5) said about him:

(He) was no insignificant person . . . (his) memory is kept green to this day by the numerous Schreber Associations which flourish especially in Saxony. . . . His activities in favour of promoting the harmonious upbringing of the young, of securing co-ordination between educators in the home and in the school, of introducing physical culture and manual work with a view to raising the standards of health—all this exerted a lasting influence upon his contemporaries.

His great reputation as the founder of therapeutic gymnastics in Germany is still shown by the wide circulation of his *Ärztliche Zimmergymnastik* (Medical Indoor Gymnastics) in medical circles and the numerous editions through which it has passed. (p. 51)

Possibly, he had one face for the world and another for those with whom he lived. Baumeyer (2), while in charge of a hospital near Dresden from 1946 to 1949, found this note among case records of Schreber's hospitalizations: "His father (founder of the Schreber Gardens in Leipzig) suffered from obsessional ideas with murderous impulses" (my translation). Baumeyer thinks its source was a member of the Schreber family or a person close to the family (Niederland, 17); the father had died thirty years before the note was written.

Dr. Schreber had two sons. Daniel Gustav, his elder son, three years older than the author of the *Memoirs*, shot and killed himself at thirty-eight

(Niederland, 18). Daniel Gustav's sister thought he had had a "progressive psychosis" before his suicide (Baumeyer, 2).

Little is known about Dr. Schreber's wife, their other children (three daughters), or their family life. We know some of Dr. Schreber's ideas about family life.

When the man can support his opinions by reason of demonstrable truth, no wife with common sense and good will will want to oppose his decisive voice. (D. G. M. Schreber, 23, p. 31)

If one wants a planned upbringing based on principles to flourish, the father above anyone else must hold the reins of upbringing in his hands. . . . The main responsibility for the whole result of upbringing always belongs to the father. . . ." (23, p. 32)

FATHER'S MORALS

Few people have been brought up according to such strict moral principles as I. . . .
—Schreber in his *Memoirs*

Dr. Schreber thought that parents must curtail their children's freedom by harsh disciplines. It was for the sake of health: moral, mental, and physical. He seemed to believe that children are criminal or ill from the start, or surely would become so, unless rescued in time.

His model of the human mind is simple. Thoughts, feelings, and acts are either good, noble, high, right, and fine; or bad, ignoble, low, wrong, and crude. Those that are neither are "indifferent."

He presumes to know what is good, noble, high, right, and fine, and what is not; he does not say how he knows. He considers sensual desires "bad." Bad elements of the mind are "weeds" to be "uprooted" and "exterminated."

Moral will power is the sword of victory in the struggle for life itself . . . without fight there is no victory. . . . We should give our children the weapon to enter this fight. (23, p. 135)

He thinks it critical to start training early. With babies of five to six months parents must follow the "law of habituation," "the most general law for mental education of this age group":

Suppress *everything* in the child, keep everything away from him which he should not make his own but guide him perseveringly towards everything to which he should habituate himself.

If we habituate the child to the Good and Right we prepare him to do the Good and the Right later with consciousness and out of free will. . . . The habit is only a necessary precondition to make possible and facilitate the proper aim of self-determination of free will. . . . If one lets the wrongly directed habits take root the child is easily put in danger; even if he later recognizes the Better he will not have the power anymore to suppress the wrongly directed habit. . . . (23, p. 60)

A stitch in time saves nine. If one does one's work early and well, one needs to do none, or nearly none, later. One will be able to leave the children to follow "freely" what they have been taught.

Compare what his son said years later:

> The fundamental view I gained about God's relation to His creation is this: God executed His power of miracles on our earth . . . only until the ultimate aim of His creation was attained with the creation of the human being. From then on He left the created organic world as it were to itself, and interfered directly by miracles only very rarely, if at all, in very exceptional cases. (19, p. 191)

The father aims to implant "self-determination," "self-reliance," and "free will." His psycho-logic is peculiar; parents must suppress the child in order to teach him self-determination. He has no faith that a child could learn when and how to regulate his own behavior without being forced to.

The *exact* opposite of what he intended occurred with his son. The psychiatrist who was superintendent of the asylum in which Schreber was confined years later wrote in a report that Schreber had *no "unimpaired self-determination* or sensible reasoning, rather the patient was completely under the power of overwhelming pathological influences" (Addenda to *Memoirs,* p. 278).

Dr. Schreber gives details of his methods:

> One must look at the moods of the little ones which are announced by screaming without reason and crying. . . . If one has convinced oneself that no real need, no disturbing or painful condition, no sickness is present, one can be assured that the screaming is only and simply the expression of a mood, a whim, the first appearance of self-will. . . . One has to step forward in a positive manner: by quick distraction of the attention, stern words, threatening gestures, rapping against the bed . . . or when all this is of no avail—by moderate, intermittent, bodily admonishments consistently repeated until the child calms down or falls asleep. . . .

> Such a procedure is necessary only once or at most twice and—one is *master* of the child *forever.* From now on a glance, a word, a single threatening gesture, is sufficient to rule the child. One should keep in mind that one shows the child the greatest kindness in this in that one saves him from many hours of tension which hinder him from thriving and also frees him from all those inner spirits of torment which very easily grow up vigorously into more serious and insurmountable enemies of life. (23, pp. 60–61)

The parent-child relationship he strives for is like the relationship between a hypnotist and the person he has put in a trance. Laing and Esterson (10) ask:

> Is the pre-psychotic child in some sense hypnotized by the parents, or is hypnosis an experimentally induced model psychosis, or, perhaps more precisely, an experimentally induced model pre-psychotic relationship? Experimental hypnosis

certainly simulates some aspects of the pre-psychotic child-parent relationship. . . . (p. 73n)

Dr. Schreber presupposes that a parent's goal is to master his child. The child must be mastered in order to be saved from *his* view of a child's self. *He* sees "tensions" and "inner spirits of torment" in a child who cries, which *he* thinks are precursors of "insurmountable enemies of life." This is how he justifies "saving" the child. He sees the child's crying as "crying without reason" because he sees no reason for it. The child could be crying because he is bored and wants someone to play with him. *He* thinks a "whim" in a five- or six-month-old is a bad sign. He does not see that an infant's wish to win a response to his whims could be a real need.

A psychoanalytic interpretation would be that Dr. Schreber projects "inner spirits of torment" from inside himself into a child; that is, he thinks he wants to master a child but really wants to master "bad" parts of himself. Many psychoanalysts have dwelled upon the motives of the person who projects: few have pondered the experience of the person *upon whom* someone else projects parts of himself, which he tries to master "in" the other person, for which he imagines is the other's sake.[3] Here is Schreber's experience of it: *"God Himself was on my side in His fight against me"* (19, p. 79n).

Everywhere Dr. Schreber talks of parents changing children, and nowhere of parents learning from children. The channel of effects is one-way. Schreber says:

A long time ago I formulated the idea that God cannot learn by experience . . . as follows: "Every attempt at an educative influence directed outwards must be given up as hopeless." (p. 155)

To educate his father, he would have had to see that his father was beset by "tensions," "inner spirits of torment," and "insurmountable enemies," why he was so beset, and how to help his father to see it—not an easy job for a child.

Although children have no effect upon parents in Dr. Schreber's system, parents are not independent of their children. Parents are not free not to fight their children's badness. Indeed, since what they are fighting is in themselves (if they resemble Dr. Schreber), how could they be free?

The father says:

If the child is lifted from the bed and carried around each time he makes noises—without checking if there is really something wrong—and is calmed by gentleness of one kind or another, this may often lead to the appearance of the emotion of spite later in the life of the child. I wish mothers and nursemaids would recognise the importance of this point! (23, p. 61)

[3] Psychoanalysts who have studied the experience of persons who have been objects of others' projections are the "neo-Freudians"—Harry Stack Sullivan, Karen Horney, Erich Fromm, and R. D. Laing.

He employs the term "spite" against a child who refuses a position his parent assigns him. In his view, the child who shows spite is bad: the child a parent can rule by "a glance," "a word," "a single threatening gesture" is good. Since he gives no evidence that lifting an infant and carrying him around whenever he makes noises may "often lead" to "spite" later—nor does any exist as far as I know—I assume what he fears is his delusion.

Another important rule: even allowed desires of the child should be fulfilled only if they are expressed in a friendly, harmless, or at least quiet, manner, never if by screaming or unruly movements . . . even if the child's need for his regular feeding is the cause. . . . One has to keep from the child even the faintest glimmer that he could, by screaming or unruly behaviour, force anything from his environment . . . the child learns very soon that only by . . . self-control he gains his purpose. (23, p. 62)

Is a five- or six-month-old free to choose to express his wants "quietly," as Dr. Schreber seems to think? An infant at this age is physiologically unable to specify some needs, especially hunger, sometimes, without screaming or waving his arms and legs; a demand for "self-control" would frustrate and confuse him. If his appeals were not endorsed, he might stop trying. Dr. Schreber says that "service personnel seldom have enough comprehension" to share these ideas of his and practice them. Maybe they comprehended more than he did.

By the last mentioned habit the child has already a noticeable headstart in the art of waiting and is ready for . . . an even more important one, the art of self-denial. . . . Each forbidden desire—whether or not it is to the child's disadvantage—must be consistently and unfailingly opposed by an unconditional refusal. The refusal of a desire alone is not enough though; one has to see to it that the child receives this refusal calmly, and if necessary, one has to make this calm acceptance a firm habit by using a stern word or threat, etc. Never make an exception from this! . . . This is the only way to make it easy for the child to attain the salutary and indispensable habit of subordination and control of his will. . . . (23, p. 63)

Why is it "salutary" and "indispensable" that a child before the age of one learn how to subordinate his will and receive calmly the denial of his desires? Dr. Schreber does not say. Perhaps this is how *his* father taught him "self-denial" when *he* was an infant. Or was it his mother, or nurse?

He could be sadistic in pursuing his high-minded goals. Consider this regimen to train a child before the age of one in "self-denial." No one must give the child a morsel of food besides the regular three meals a day. His nurse must seat him on her lap while she eats or drinks whatever she wishes. However much the child should wish food or drink, she must give him none.

"Here is only a small experience from my own family circle. The nurse of one of my children, generally a very sweet person, once gave a child something between his meals even though having been told explicitly not to. . . . It was a piece of pear which she herself was eating. . . . She was without any other reason dismissed from the service at once because I had lost the necessary trust in her unconditional correctness." (23, p. 64)

News about the episode spread among the children's nurses in Leipzig and from then on, he says, he had "no further trouble with any other such erring maids or nurses."

Dr. Schreber's method of teaching a baby self-denial is to set up a hierarchy by which he applies his power upon the nurse to apply hers upon the baby. Only the baby is denied anything. It is relevant that Schreber, in his "nervous illness" many years later, experienced God as a hierarchy of powers.

Here is another example Dr. Schreber gives from his family. Since he is talking of a male infant, he could be referring to the author of the *Memoirs:*

One of my children had fallen ill at the age of one-and-a-half and the only treatment, though a dangerous one, giving any hope for saving his life was possible only through the completely quiet submissiveness of the young patient. It succeeded, because the child had been accustomed from the beginning to the most absolute obedience toward me, whereas otherwise the child's life would in all probability have been beyond any chance of rescue. (23, p. 67)

It would be interesting to know how the child's absolute obedience toward his father made possible the only treatment that could save his life, and what that treatment was. It is unlikely we can ever find out.

A parent's demand does not always need a rationale, he thinks, as in the next example. Might makes right.

If one asks a child to hand something to oneself with one specific hand but the child will use only the other hand, the intelligent upbringer will not rest until the act is done as demanded and the impure motive is removed. (23, p. 137)

The irrelevance of the parent's demand is irrelevant to Dr. Schreber. He never considers it possible that a child who opts to disobey a parent's arbitrary wish may know, better than his parent, what is best for him.

In his view, a parent must do more than control a child's acts. He must control his "*sentiments,*" his "*motives.*" The "outer" is less important than the "inner."

Let us always treat the child exactly as his sentiments, which are mirrored so clearly in the whole of his being, deserve. . . . If parents stay true to themselves with this principle, they will soon be rewarded by the appearance of a wonderful relationship where the child is nearly always ruled merely by parental eye movements. (23, pp. 137–38)

Dr. Schreber seems to be saying that as parents raise their power over their children, they will be "rewarded" by the possibility of greater power still; the goal is for the child to be in a sort of trance in which he experiences each glance of the parent as a command. Why is that relationship wonderful? And for whom?

Although Dr. Schreber thinks the child must be rewarded or punished not only for his acts, but for the sentiments underlying them, he thinks the child must not obey in order to get praise or reward. He thinks a wish for praise or reward is a "degraded" and "impure" sentiment. Nor must the child obey because he fears punishment. *And* he must not obey while secretly *wishing* to disobey; that would be dishonesty—a bad sentiment. He must obey because he knows it is right to obey, no matter how whimsical his parent's wish.

To tailor his consciousness to meet the demands of this system, a child would have to deny, repress, split, project, displace, etc., much of his experience. Even having done so, it is hard to see how in some situations he could think any thought without breaking a rule.

Schreber in his *Memoirs* says that God, whom he experiences as irresistibly attracted to him, is able to withdraw from him only when he, Schreber, stops thinking. He may be remembering his relationship with his father without realizing it; to realize it would be to think a forbidden thought. The father sought to crush so many thoughts in children that his son might have thought, had he been allowed to think it, that his father would leave him alone only if he stopped thinking.

Frequently, Dr. Schreber advises parents to make their children unaware of their own experience if it is of a sort he thinks is bad. He tells parents to stage this scene with their three- to five-year-old children as a training exercise after punishing them; the aim is to induce the children to feel what he thinks they should.

It is generally salutary for the sentiments if the child after each punishment, after he has recovered, is gently prodded (preferably by a third person) to offer to shake the hand of the punisher as a sign of a plea for forgiveness. . . . From then on everything should be forgotten.

After this prodding has occurred a few times the child, feeling his duty, will freely approach the punisher. This ensures against the possibility of residual spiteful or bitter feelings and mediates the feeling of repentance (the next goal of punishment) and the benefit that results from it, and generally gives the child the salutary impression that he still owes the punisher something, not the other way around, even if maybe a word or a blow more than necessary should have befallen the child. Generally, any plea for love must come from the child, and only from the child. . . . If one forgets about the repentance process here one risks always that the main aim of each punishment, the true serious feeling of repentance, will not be reached but instead a kernel of bitter feeling will stay stuck in the depths of children's hearts. If one were to omit this procedure altogether one would permit the punished child the right of anger against the punisher which is certainly not consistent with an intelligent pedagogic approach. (23, p. 142)

To clarify all Dr. Schreber's implicit premises here, and other premises that these imply, would take us off our course. Briefly, here are a few that are apparent:

Punishment of a child is proof of his guilt. Although punishment can be excessive, it can never be unwarranted. Its aim is to bring about an acknowledgment of guilt which he calls "repentance."

It is a child's duty, not his choice, to ask for forgiveness. He is not allowed not to ask to be forgiven, i.e., he cannot harbor a feeling that he has been punished unfairly, even if he has, or, feeling he has been fairly punished, to endure his feelings privately and to cope with them as he wishes.

Only the punisher can forgive a punished child.

One acts in the light of what one sees. Each of these premises is a constraint by which Dr. Schreber limits his vision. He forces the child's view to fit his view of what the child's view should be. This he can do only by altering the child's experience. Any "spite," "bitterness," or "anger" the child feels toward his punisher must be repressed.

Repression, in the psychoanalytic view, is an *intra*personal defense built to ward off real, imagined, or fantasied harm. Freud said that a person represses experience if he fears it may lead him to act in ways for which he remembers (or imagines, or fantasies) he has been punished, or for which he perceives (or imagines, or fantasies) he will be punished. Repression can also be a *trans*personal maneuver. I am distinguishing one's operation upon another's experience (transpersonal) from one's operation upon one's own (intrapersonal).

A person (often a parent) orders another person (often a child) to forget thoughts, feelings, or acts that the first person cannot, or will not, allow in the other. This is standard practice in some relationships (especially in families with a schizophrenic offspring). If the first person's aim is to protect himself from experience of which he fears the other may remind him, if the other experiences too much, the order serves as a transpersonal *defense*. A transpersonal defense can be an *attack* on another person's experience.

Dr. Schreber recommends repression as a transpersonal maneuver. It could have served as a transpersonal defense for him if he feared *his* *un*-"repentant" feelings toward his parents. His son thought that someone might think God could resort to what I am calling transpersonal defenses:

Whoever has taken the trouble of reading the above attentively may spontaneously have thought that God Himself must have been or be in a precarious position, if the conduct of a single human being could endanger Him in any way and even if He Himself, if only in limited instances, could be enticed into a kind of *conspiracy against human beings who are fundamentally innocent*. (19, P. 59)

Later, he says he "had become a danger to God Himself" (p. 75). In a postscript to his book he notes:

God is a living Being and would Himself have to be ruled by egoistic motives, if other living beings existed who could endanger Him or in some way be detrimental to his interests. (p. 251)

Is he ascribing operations to his father's mind in order to explain his father's behavior, without naming him?

FREUD'S ANALYSIS

In his analysis of Schreber, Freud chose as data certain of Schreber's conscious experiences. To explain his data—Schreber's conscious experiences—he inferred that Schreber had had other experiences of which Schreber was unaware, and of which he kept himself unaware by operations of which he also was unaware.

He saw Schreber as paranoid. In his paper on Schreber (5) he said:

What lies at the core of the conflict in cases of paranoia among males is a homosexual wishful phantasy of *loving a man*. . . .

Freud thought that the paranoid man contradicts his love for a man by hating a man and replaces "internal perceptions—feelings—" by "external perceptions."

Consequently the proposition "I hate him" becomes transformed by *projection* into another one: "*He hates* (persecutes) *me*, which will justify me in hating him." And thus the impelling unconscious feeling makes its appearance as though it were the consequence of an external perception: "I do not *love* him—I *hate* him, because HE PERSECUTES ME." (pp. 62–63, italics in the original)

To paraphrase Freud, if a man loves a man and feels he is forbidden to, he denies his love and changes it to its opposite; "I love him" becomes "I hate him" by denial and reversal. If he feels forbidden to hate a man, he changes his hatred to its inverse: "I hate him" becomes "He hates me" by projection. A man who thinks he is persecuted reaches that position by making three operations upon his homosexual love: denial, reversal, and projection. These steps keep him unaware of "bad" feelings. He is unconscious of loving a man, of the steps he takes to keep himself unconscious, and, I presume, of his motives for keeping the love unconscious and for keeping the steps to keep it unconscious, unconscious.

Whether Freud's theory explains why some men feel persecuted I do not know. His theory of why Schreber felt persecuted neglects much of what probably occurred between Schreber and his father.

Given what can be reasonably inferred about how the father treated his sons, it is likely that they would have *hated* him if they could have. The father taught parents to stop children from feeling "spite," "anger," and "bitterness" toward their parents; these feelings can be classed as *hatred*. Therefore, his sons may have needed to be concerned with how not to hate their father. Karl Menninger (14), referring to Freud's analysis of Schreber, said:

> The man who feels himself persecuted is obviously defending himself not against his love of someone so much as against his hate for someone, someone whom the persecutor represents. He defends himself by saying, "It is not I who hate him, but he who hates me."

His conclusion, reached by reasoning unlike mine, is compatible with my findings.

Of course, in Freud's view, to hate or love someone means to hate *and* love him. Did Schreber fear his love for his father? Perhaps; however, I see no need to assume it, for his feelings of persecution can be adequately explained as *transforms* of his *real* persecution.

PARANOIA AND PERSECUTION

Dr. Schreber told parents to persecute their children. He does not seem to have seen it as persecution himself.

Consider a matrix with two columns and two rows, yielding four possibilities:

One is not persecuted and (1) knows it, (2) does not know it (that is, one thinks one is persecuted when one is not).

One is persecuted and (3) knows it (4) does not know it.

The first position is "normal." The second is ascribed by psychiatrists to people they call paranoid. What of the last two, especially the fourth? There is no term in psychiatric usage, or in English, for "is persecuted without knowing it." Since there is no name for this condition, one can suffer from it without risk of being labeled.

(Note: When I say "is persecuted," I also mean *has been* persecuted. Some persons, persecuted by parents in childhood, are also persecuted by them in adulthood. Some unwittingly find, or induce, others to persecute them, often in ways remarkably similar to their childhood experience. And many, like Schreber, are persecuted by *memories* of past persecution.)

I think many people whom psychiatrists call "paranoid" have been persecuted, and know it, but they do not recognize their real persecutors, nor how they have been persecuted. They belong to the last two groups. To call them paranoid, which presupposes that they are not "really" persecuted but imagine it, is false and misleading.

What is clinically called paranoia is often the partial realization—as through a glass darkly—that one has been or is persecuted. One may never have realized it before. "Paranoid" thoughts can be *images* of events that originally, days or decades earlier, were seen, heard, felt, smelled, or tasted.

Paranoia (*para*—beside, beyond + *nous*—mind) means literally the state of being besides, or out of, one's mind. If a person called paranoid sees the truth that he is persecuted (without seeing by whom, or how), he is partly "in" his mind; the label is partly a misnomer. It is ironic that one may be regarded as ill for the first time in one's life, just upon emergence from a lifelong, deeper ignorance.

Some people do not see who their real persecutors are or the methods of persecution, because their persecutors do not let them. The persecutors may persuade or force their victims to see their persecution as love, especially if they are the parents, siblings, spouses, or children of their victims. It is easier for the persecutors to lie if they believe the lies are true. The persecutor may see his persuasion or force as an act of love also, and may try to convince his victim of it.

Here is a schema that is simpler than family life *in vivo* ever is:

Parent persecutes child.

Parent sees parent's persecution as love.

Child sees parent's persecution as persecution.

Child may or may not see that parent sees his persecution of child as love: usually he does not.

Parent wants child to love, honor, and obey parent, for child's sake. If child does not, parent must force child to, for child's sake.

The more child sees parent's persecution as persecution, the more parent persecutes child and sees his persecution as love.

Child tries to conceal that he sees parent's persecution as persecution, and to conceal that he is concealing anything.

Parent tells child: "Dishonesty is wicked. I will punish you, for your own good, if you lie."

A variation is: "You *cannot* hide your feelings from me."

I am distinguishing "You should not hide your feelings from me" from "You *cannot* hide your feelings from me." The first is an order; the second an attribution that masks an order. The second is like the hypnotist's induction and is a stronger technique of control, probably because the order is hidden. For more discussion of this point, see Laing (11, pp. 11–14) and Haley (7, pp. 20–40).

Child sees that parent will persecute child most if parent sees that child sees parent's persecution as persecution, and is concealing that he is, and is concealing that he is concealing anything.

Child conceals from *himself* that he sees that Parent persecutes him, and conceals from *himself* that he is concealing anything.

If this schema, or one like it, summarizes some of what has occurred between some "paranoid" people, when they were children, and their parents, it would shed light on why they so mistrust others. It would also explain Robert Knight's finding (8) that ascribing homosexual wishes to a "paranoid" patient "not only does not relieve the patient but often makes him more paranoid than ever" (quoted by Macalpine and Hunter, 13, p. 23).

Substitute son for child and father for parent. I deduce from my study of Schreber's father's ideas that this situation, or one like it, existed between father and son.

The writings of the father and son show that what the father saw as love, his son saw as persecution. Note the opposite values each gives to "rays":

Father says:

Once the childish mind is completely penetrated by *love* and *respect* and all the warm *rays* which gush forth from them, the will of the child is ruled more and more from this perspective and is led gently towards the pure and noble direction. (23, p. 235)

Son says:

In itself a state of affairs must be considered contrary to the Order of the World in which the *rays* serve mainly to *inflict damage* on the body of a single human being or to play tricks with the objects with which he is occupied—such harmless miracles have become particularly frequent latterly. (19, p. 132)

Naturally I am referring only to *my own case,* that is to say a case in which God entered into continual contact by *rays* with a single human being, a contact which could no longer be severed and which therefore was contrary to the Order of the World. (19, p. 153)

Father and son use the same word, *strahlen,* translated as "rays."

Schreber feels harassed by God's attraction to him and would like God to withdraw from him, a perfectly intelligible wish in view of his father's behavior toward him as a child. He is not attrac*ted* to God, as Freud thought; he is attrac*tive,* and would like not to be. It is not "I love him" that bothers him, but "He loves me."

In his report of Schreber's hospital records, Baumeyer (2) says that Schreber "often declared that he had to put up a strong resistance *against* 'the homosexual *love* of certain persons.' "

This passage of the father links with the last steps of my schema:

If one does not secure in the child's heart adherence to truth by imprinting of a *holy fear,* of each glimmer of untruth, how can one wonder when later in life, with thousands of temptations to lie frequently demanding one's whole power to resist, the domination of the lie spreads its rule, already having been prepared in youth . . . *the child should be permeated by the feeling of the impossibility of locking up something in his heart knowingly and permanently from you. Without this unconditional openheartedness, any upbringing will lack a safe foundation.* But to get there an additional condition must be fulfilled. You have to come to the help of the child so that he can take in and secure the courage often necessary to hold strictly to the truth, i.e., this means in the case of a freely offered, open and full confession of guilt the guilt must be judged and punished recognizably more mildly, taking account of the openness, but in the opposite case the guilt is punished onefold, the untruth connected with it is punished tenfold. (23, pp. 144-45)

This is how an able persecutor controlled his victims in the name of truth, openheartedness, and courage. Big Brother was incarnate long before Orwell wrote *1984.*

Many psychiatrists and psychoanalysts have said that the people they call schizophrenic suffer from an inability to distinguish "I" from not-"I," that they lack "ego boundaries." I suggest that some of these people have been taught by their families that they should not, or cannot, live with an "I," as Schreber's father apparently taught him. Note that Dr. Schreber does not say children should not keep things from their parents; he says they should be "permeated by the feeling of the *impossibility*" of it; that is, they must feel that they *cannot.*

What the German playwright Lessing said could apply to a man brought up by Dr. Schreber's methods: "A man who does not lose his reason over certain things can have no reason to lose."

THE CONTEXT

Nearly everyone who has studied families of persons labeled schizophrenic agrees that the irrationality of the schizophrenic finds its rationality in the context of his first family. In what context does that family context find *its* rationality? What is the social network around the family of a schizophrenic, and what are its properties? (see Speck, 26) Where do the patterns of thought, word, and deed of parents of mad offspring fit in? We would be wise, I think, to confess we do not know.

A man renowned as a great pedagogue—Freud said his activities "exerted a lasting influence on his contemporaries"—has two sons. One kills himself and the other goes mad. In what social context can Dr. Schreber's system of child rearing find its rationality? Why was his system so highly esteemed? Inasmuch as his *Medical Indoor Gymnastics* (25) has sold nearly forty editions and is translated in seven languages, his behavior has been part of a very large network indeed. Remember that Hitler and his peers were raised when Dr. Schreber's books, preaching household totalitarianism, were popular.

Much scholarship has been devoted to understanding Schreber; all of it until recently ignored his father's writings as data. Why?

Schreber says, *"God did not really understand the living human being . . ."* (19, p. 75, italics in the original). This is the closest he comes to telling the plain truth about his father. Why did no one else get closer? Possibly, had he seen the truth about his childhood, he would have found no one to appreciate what he saw.

Schreber's father was a key figure in a conspiracy of certain German parents against their children. The conspirators did not see themselves as conspirators. Were they treating their children as their parents had treated them?

Edwin Lemert (12), an American sociologist who studied the interpersonal networks around people considered paranoid, found that

The general idea that the paranoid person symbolically fabricates the conspiracy against him is in our own estimation incorrect or incomplete. Nor can we agree that he lacks insight, as is so frequently claimed. To the contrary, many paranoid persons properly realize that they are being isolated and excluded by concerted interaction, or that they are being manipulated. However, they are at a loss to estimate accurately or realistically the dimensions and form of the coalition arrayed against them.

Schreber was born into a conspiracy against him. Those who tried, while he lived and after he died, to render his experience intelligible failed to see the conspiracy. In failing to see the conspiracy, they sustained it unwittingly. We need to know how to render *their* failure intelligible.

ADDENDUM

I am not alone in intuiting a possible link between the micro-social despotism of the Schreber family and the macro-social despotism of Nazi Germany. Elias Canetti (4), a novelist and sociologist, also did. He does not know of my views of Schreber's father (nor did I know of his ideas about Schreber when I wrote this paper), and he does not mention Schreber's father; he thinks of the link with Nazism, using only the *Memoirs* as data. He says Schreber gives us

a very distinct picture of God: he is a despot and nothing else. His realm contains provinces and factions. "God's interests," as they are bluntly and summarily designated, demand the increase of his power. This, and this only, is why he would not deny any human being the share of blessedness due to him; human beings who hinder him are done away with. (p. 444)

Later, Canetti says:

As no-one today is likely to deny, his (Schreber's) political system had within a few decades been accorded high honour: though in a rather cruder and less literate form it became the creed of a great nation, leading . . . to the conquest of Europe and coming within a hair's breadth of the conquest of the world. Thus Schreber's claims were posthumously vindicated by his unwitting disciples. We are not likely to accord him the same recognition, but the amazing and incontrovertible likeness between the two systems may serve to justify the time we have devoted to this single case of paranoia; . . . (p. 447)

REFERENCES

1. Ashby, R. A., *An Introduction to Cybernetics*, London, Chapman and Hall, 1956.

2. Baumeyer, F., "The Schreber Case," *Int. J. Psychoanal.*, 37: 61–74, 1956.

3. Bleuler, E., *Dementia Praecox or The Group of Schizophrenias*, New York, International Universities Press, 1950.

4. Canetti, E., *Masse und Macht*, Hamburg, Claassen Verlag, 1960. Translated as *Crowds and Power* by C. Stewart, London, Victor Gollancz, 1962.

5. Freud, S., "Psycho-Analytic Notes on an Autobiographical Account of a Case of Paranoia (Dementia Paranoides)," *The Standard Edition of the Complete Psychological Works of Sigmund Freud*, Vol. XII, London, Hogarth Press, 1958.

6. Haley, J., "The Family of the Schizophrenic: A Model System," *J. Nerv. Ment. Dis.*, 129: 357–74, 1959.

7. ———, *Strategies of Psychotherapy*, New York, Grune & Stratton, 1963.

8. Knight, R. P., "The Relationship of Latent Homosexuality to the Mechanism of Paranoid Delusions," *Bull. Menninger Clinc*, 4: 149–59, 1940.

9. Lacan, J., "L'instance de la lettre dans l'inconscient ou la raison depuis Freud," La Psychanalyse, III: 47–81, 1957. Translated as "The Insistence of the Letter in the Unconscious," in *Structuralism*, Ehrmann, J. (Ed.), New York, Doubleday, Anchor Books, 1970.

10. Laing, R. D. and Esterson, A., *Sanity, Madness and The Family*, London, Tavistock Publications, 1964.

11. Laing, R. D., *The Politics of the Family*, Massey Lectures, Eighth Series, Canada Canadian Broadcasting Corporation, 1969.

12. Lemert, E. M., "Paranoia and the Dynamics of Exclusion," *Sociometry*, 25: 2–20, 1962.

13. MacAlpine, I. and Hunter, R. A., See Schreber, D. P.

14. Menninger, K., *Love Against Hate*, New York, Harcourt Brace, 1942.

15. Niederland, W. G., "The 'Miracled-Up' World of Schreber's Childhood," *Psychoanal. Stud. Child*, 14: 383–413, 1959.

16. ———, "Schreber: Father and Son," *Psychoanal. Quarterly*, 28: 151–69, 1959.

17. ———, "Schreber's Father," *J. Am. Psychoanal. Assn.*, 8: 492–99, 1960.

18. ———, "Further Data and Memorabilia Pertaining to the Schreber Case," *Int. J. Psychoanal.*, 44: 201–7, 1963.

19. Schreber, D. P., *Dentwürdigkeiten eines Nervenkranken*, Leipzig, Oswald, Mutze, 1903. Translated and edited by MacAlpine, I. and Hunter, R. A., *Memoirs of My Nervous Illness*, London, Dawson & Son, 1955.

20. Schreber, D. G. M., *Das Buch der Gesundheit* (The Book of Health), Leipzig, H. Fries, 1839.

21. ———, *Dis Eigentumlichkeiten des Kindlichen Organismus* (The Characteristics of the Child's Organism), Leipzig, Fleischer, 1852.

22. ———, *Die Schädlichen Korperhaltungen und Gewohnheiten der Kinder nebst Angabe*

der Mittel Dagegen (The Harmful Body Positions and Habits of Children including a Statement of Counteracting Measures), Leipzig, Fleischer, 1853.

23. ———, *Kallipädie oder Erziehung zur Schonheit durch Naturgetreue und Gleichmassige Förderung Normaler Körperbildung* (Education Towards Beauty by Natural and Balanced Furtherance of Normal Body Growth), Leipzig, Fleischer, 1858.

24. ———, *Die Planmässige Schärfung der Sinnesorgane* (The Systematically Planned Sharpening of the Sense Organs), Leipzig, Fleischer, 1859.

25. ———, *Medical Indoor Gymnastics*, 26th ed., Leipzig, Fleischer, and London, Williams & Norgate, 1899.

26. Speck, R., "Psychotherapy of the Social Network of a Schizophrenic Family," Paper presented at the American Psychological Association Symposium on "Conjoint Family Therapy and Assessment," New York, New York, September 6, 1966.

9

MENTAL DISEASES IN CHINA
AND THEIR TREATMENT
Ruth Sidel

Reliable information on the Chinese Communist society is difficult to obtain. Chapter 9, which is based on Ruth Sidel's recent trip to China, is the best discussion available of the Chinese Communist approach to "mental illness." It documents the extensive use of group techniques alluded to in the Introduction to this volume and in Chapter 7.

INTRODUCTION

The material in this paper is based on observations made during a one-month visit by my husband and me to the People's Republic of China in September-October, 1971 as the guests of the Chinese Medical Association.

Reprinted by permission of the Fogarty International Center, NIH, and the author.

To understand in depth a society whose history, culture, and organization is vastly different from one's own is impossible in such a brief period of time. What we did attempt was to glimpse some of China's problems, goals, and solutions. Looking at Chinese mental-health facilities is a particularly difficult task, for many of the premises involved in their psychiatric care differ greatly from ours in the West. For those of us trained in Freudian thinking, the task involves putting our assumptions to one side, for a time, and examining a very different view of man and his psyche. Of crucial importance in the Chinese view of man is the belief in man's ability to change, given a sympathetic environment and "education and reeducation." Underpinning this view, and in fact running through all activities in the society, is politics. As our Chinese hosts frequently told us, "We put politics in command." And as we shall see, politics is in command in the area of mental health.

The organization of Chinese society today must be considered in any discussion of mental health. It seems to be a society of great consensus: similar customs and mores apply to vast numbers of the population. Basic needs such as food, clothing, housing, jobs, education and medical care are now guaranteed to essentially the entire population, albeit at a minimal level. No one is left to fend for himself; the population both in the cities and in the countryside is divided into small units characterized by both self-reliance and mutual help. The individual is expected to work hard and participate extensively in local affairs, but is also cared for by his family, neighbors, or associates at work when he is in need of such care. In addition, there is no doubt little tolerance for asocial or antisocial behavior, and great pressure is undoubtedly applied to assure conformity to the approved way of life.

Our view of Chinese mental-health services was extremely limited. We visited the psychiatric department of the Third Peking Hospital and the Shanghai Mental Hospital. We talked with doctors, nurses, and members of the Revolutionary Committees of both hospitals at some length. We also were able to gather general information about the structure of Chinese society and its relationship to mental health from our hosts of the Chinese Medical Association.

THE "BITTER PAST"

Long before Western psychiatric theories entered Chinese medical thinking, there were two divergent streams of thought that explained mental illness: the philosophical or medical approach, and folk beliefs and folk medical practices. Both of these streams of thought had great impact on modern Chinese psychiatric thinking.

To look initially at the philosophical or medical body of thought, according to ancient Chinese medical writings, all disease including mental illness was caused by an imbalance of two forces: the Yin and the Yang. According to Ilza Veith, "These two forces which stand for the negative and the positive, the dark and the white, the moon and the sun, the noxious and the beneficial, also denote the female and male elements, both of which are ever present in man and woman alike. Disease arises when the proportions of the two elements begin to vary from the normal" (1). The imbalance between the Yin and the Yang was thought to be caused by deviation from the Tao, or the "Way," which provided the guide for all morality and human conduct. The Tao can be further thought of as being an "ethical superstructure" that "provided for all eventualities in life and for all essential types of interpersonal relationships" (1). Once transgression against this ethical superstructure occurred, the way to a return to health was through a return to Tao.

Although there is no supernatural element in the philosophical or medical explanations of mental illness, the popular or folk beliefs about the origins of mental illness are based almost entirely on supernatural causes. And although the believers in Tao saw the mind and the body as indivisible, popular beliefs saw the mind and the body as separate entities. Spirits and demons were thought from earliest times to be responsible for many of the ills that befell man. Spirits were thought to be everywhere: "in the water, the caves, the trees and graves, they lurked in the soil and under rocks. They swarmed about the homes of men, in populated as well as in isolated regions and, according to many tales, their favorite abodes were the privies, where man is alone and helpless and flight difficult." (2) Once a demon or spirit entered a person and made him ill, they had to be exorcised. The first exorcists were members of a priesthood called *Wu*, which to the present day has the meaning of wizard, witch, expeller of demons. *Wu* is first encountered in the "Rites of the Chou dynasty" (1122–255 B.C.), and it eventually became synonymous with the word for physician, *Wu-i*, meaning "magical physician" (2). The *wu*, who might be either male or female, was thought to be able to cure because he had a greater proportion of Yang than ordinary people. To exorcise the spirit or demon that had entered the sick person, the *Wu* might put the patient into a deep sleep, might dance around the ill person, and was likely to inflict wounds upon himself as a method of cure.

Among the spirits that might enter a person, the spirits of the dead were greatly feared, particularly the spirits of those who had not had proper funeral observances or those who had died through violence. It was thought that the spirits of the dead could steal the souls of the living particularly while the living were asleep and the soul was occupied with dreams. Because the spirits of the dead were thought to be so powerful, much of the work of the medical priests lay in attempting to appease their hostility. One particular group of spirits were thought to be especially powerful, the T'ien Ku, otherwise known as "Celestial Dog." They were thought to be able to speak to their victims, inflict amnesia upon them, and particularly disturb young sons.

The fox was also thought to have great powers, in the folklore of both China and Japan. He was thought to be so powerful that he could not only bring on mental disease but could also impersonate those who could cure mental illness, thereby causing massive confusion. During the Han Dynasty and the Han period of literature (206 B.C.–280 A.D.), the fear of foxes was widespread (2). The fox seems to have played a great role in sexual seductions and assaults, sometimes occupying the bodies of young women and sometimes of men. The following passage from the *Hsuan-chung-chi*, written in the first few centuries A.D., demonstrates the power the fox was thought to have:

When a fox is 50 years old, it becomes a beautiful female . . . or a grown-up man who has sexual intercourse with women. Such beings are able to know things occurring at more than a thousand miles distant: they can poison men by sorcery, or possess them, and bewilder them, so that they lose their memory and knowledge. And when a fox is a thousand years old, it penetrates to heaven, and becomes a Celestial Fox. (2)

Because the mentally ill person was thought to be possessed by a spirit or demon or fox, the onset of illness was swift and the cure might be equally sudden. The *Wu* by his ministrations could exorcise the demon suddenly; swift exorcism led to a belief in the curability of mental illness that has seemed to carry through to the present. The theory of possession by demons also leads logically to the attachment of no blame to the patient himself, thereby reducing the stigma attached to mental illness.

Other popular beliefs about the origin of mental illness were that one might have been guilty of a misdeed in one's previous life; that one's ancestors might have offended the gods who are now punishing the offspring; that the god of the wind is using the insane man's home as a temporary residence and that his spirit is living in the ill person's body; that some organ inside the body is deformed or has lost its function; or that the circulation of blood within the ill person is running in the opposite direction from that of the normal person. It was felt that mental control was through the heart and that if the heart loses control, the body is then without direction (3).

These were some of the prevalent beliefs of the causes of mental illness when the first mental hospital was opened in Canton in 1897. Although it started with only 30 beds and increased in size to 500 beds, it was closed in the 1930s (1). The first Department of Neurology was established in 1921 at the Peking Union Medical College, ten years after that medical school was established (4). The growth of psychiatry and neurology in China from 1921 to 1949, the year the Communists took power, was very slow; in

1948 there were approximately 1,000 beds for psychiatric patients in all of China (4).

In 1949 there were only four psychiatric hospitals in China, one each in Peking, Shanghai, Canton, and Nanking; patients were often treated cruelly, bound to their beds, and given barely any psychiatric care (4). By the 1930s and 1940s, most people suffering from mental illness were still being kept in their homes with their families; if they were found in the street doing anything wrong they might be "thrown into prison and treated as if they were criminals. If they are harmless and wander in the streets, they are mocked and laughed at and are often stoned." (3b)

Estimates of the incidence of mental disease in China in the mid-1930s have ranged from as low as one person in every 1,000—or 400,000 mentally ill persons—to one in every 400—or 1,000,000 to 1,250,000 (3c). Widespread poverty, violence, starvation, and the brutalizing effect these conditions had on family life made for fertile ground for mental illness. The cruelty to which women were subjected—being sold into marriage at a young age, having to serve her husband's family, being treated brutally by her husband and particularly by her mother-in-law, and bearing many children, most of whom might well die—drove many women to suicide and undoubtedly drove others to mental illness.

Prior to 1949, venereal disease was an important cause of mental illness. The earliest estimates of the existence of prostitution in China are from the Chow Dynasty in 650 B.C. Venereal disease appears to have been introduced from 1488 through 1521 A.D.—during the time of the Ming Dynasty—and started from Kwangtung Province and spread to the north (3d). At the time of Liberation, the prevalence of syphilis was said to be 10 percent in the national minority areas and 5 percent in the cities (5). Although there was some effort to control and treat venereal disease, medical techniques were hindered by the popular belief that venereal disease was a logical punishment for misdeeds (3e). It was not until Liberation that the houses of prostitution were closed and venereal disease systematically rooted out and treated.

Another major cause of mental illness prior to 1949 was drug addiction. It has been estimated that there were 300,000 addicts in Peking alone in the mid-1930s (6a). In 1935, the Nationalist government launched a six-year program aimed at "the total suppression of the chronic use of morphine and heroin" within two years and opium within six years. Compulsory treatment was inaugurated; it included two to three weeks of hospitalization, followed by hard labor in Peking and Nanking to build up the addict's physical condition. There were a large percentage of relapses and in 1937 addicts began to receive severe punishment: some recidivists were executed and others were sent to prison (6b).

FROM LIBERATION TO CULTURAL REVOLUTION

From the time the Communists took power on the mainland in 1949, which they call "Liberation," until 1965, the government put great stress on medical care. By 1952—when the Chinese Society of Neurology and Psychiatry, affiliated with the Chinese Medical Association in Peking, was established—there were only 100 neuropsychiatrists in China; by 1967, this figure had risen to 436.

By 1957, the number of psychiatric beds had been increased to 20,000, and new methods of treating mentally ill patients had been introduced. Isolation and the binding of patients were prohibited, and work therapy was introduced. Before the Cultural Revolution all of the medical schools in China taught courses in psychiatry, and neuropsychiatric research was carried on widely. From 1958 through 1961, electroencephalographic research was carried on as well as research into schizophrenia (4). Psychiatric services spread at an even greater rate in China in the late 1950s and early 1960s. There have been reports of treatment of mental illnesses in the autonomous regions of Inner Mongolia and in Urumchi, the center of the Sinkiang Uighur autonomous region (4).

Before the Cultural Revolution, traditional medicine—including acupuncture, ignipuncture, breathing exercises, and the use of herb medicines—as well as Western medicine was used in the treatment of mental disease. Acupuncture will be dealt with in greater detail later in this paper. Ignipuncture is "treatment by means of thermal excitation through various methods of cautery and burning at empirically determined points of the body" (4). Sometimes acupuncture and ignipuncture were combined in a course of treatment called *Chen chu,* which dates back 2,000 years in the treatment of psychoses, neuroses, and headaches.

The breathing exercises used were similar to those used by Buddhist monks, and therapeutic results have been obtained after regular use of breathing exercises, morning and evening, for several months (4).

THE CURRENT SCENE

Since the Cultural Revolution, there has been increased emphasis in all branches of medicine on combining traditional medicine with Western medicine. Although the Chinese have been combining traditional and Western medicine since 1949 in other branches of medical care, the psychiatric sphere seems to have concentrated more on Western methods of treatment and to have neglected traditional techniques from the time of Liberation until 1965. Using the slogan, "Let the past serve the present and let the foreign serve China," Western-trained doctors have been revamping their psychiatric services to include traditional methods and political techniques adopted by the society at large since the Cultural Revolution.

As in all other institutions in China since the Cultural Revolution, the psychiatric hospital is now run by a Revolutionary Committee containing the three-in-one combination of the People's Liberation Army, cadres (political workers), and members of the mass. The mass includes those people who work in any institution; in a mental hospital, it includes the doctors, nurses, cleaning help, and auxiliary workers. The Revolutionary Committee also often includes another three-in-one combination of aged people, middle-aged people, and young people. The Revolutionary Committee at the Shanghai Mental Hospital, which was founded in 1958, is made up of 15 members, 11 men and 4 women. The hospital has 13 wards, 5 for women and 8 for men, comprising a total of 916 beds. The staff includes 61 doctors and 169 nurses. The methods currently used in treating mental illness include collective help, self-reliance, drug therapy, acupuncture, "heart-to-heart talks," follow-up care, community ethos, productive labor, and the teachings of Mao.

COLLECTIVE HELP

With the participation of members of the People's Liberation Army in the administration of hospitals since the Cultural Revolution, some psychiatric hospitals are using the Army model of organization and are dividing the patients on the wards into divisions and groups so that they can become a "collective fighting group instead of a ward." Within these "fighting groups," the patients who are getting better are paired with newer and sicker patients so that they can help each other with "mutual love and mutual help."

SELF-RELIANCE

The patients themselves are encouraged to investigate their own disease, to investigate their symptoms, and to understand their treatment. They are encouraged to study themselves in order to recognize their own condition and to prevent their own relapse.

DRUG THERAPY

Seriously ill patients are given chlorpromazine (Thorazine), though evidently in smaller doses than before the Cultural Revolution. Insulin-shock and electric-shock therapy have been eliminated since the Cultural Revolution.

ACUPUNCTURE

Three kinds of acupuncture are used for certain forms of schizophrenia: (1) acupuncture needles placed in the temples or behind or in front of the ear and hooked up to a battery box for 3 to 5 minutes at a time, once or twice a day for a 40-to-45-day course: (2) acupuncture of the ear; and (3) acupuncture on the body, on the legs, and on the arms for relief of excitement, catatonia, and depression. This third form is generally done from 15 to 20 minutes, three times a day.

"HEART-TO-HEART TALKS"

A psychiatrist meets with patients individually or in small groups at regular intervals to discuss the patients' problems and to help them understand their illness more completely. We were told that the most important form of treatment is the relationship between the psychiatrist and the patient.

FOLLOW-UP CARE

After the patient is discharged, he is followed up every two weeks and then monthly in the outpatient department. Sometimes a doctor or a nurse from the staff of the hospital will make a home visit. Before discharge, a doctor will have visited the patient's place of work and will make sure the patient returns to a job that is best for his mental health. His job has been kept for him until his return, but it may be that another task within his work unit would better suit his mental-health needs. Often, the patient is kept on chlorpromazine after discharge, but on a smaller dosage.

COMMUNITY ETHOS

Every neighborhood, both urban and rural, is organized under the direction of a Revolutionary Committee, again made up of members of the People's Liberation Army, cadres, and the mass (the people who live in the neighborhood). The elected members of the Revolutionary Committee provide the social services, mediate disputes, provide marital counseling, and in general look after the people in the neighborhood. When a patient is about to be discharged from a mental hospital, he is under the "special concern" of members of the Revolutionary Committee in his neighborhood as well as his family and friends; this community concern plus the assurance of his job and family waiting for him helps ease the transition from hospital to community.

PRODUCTIVE LABOR

As in the larger society, where all members are encouraged to do productive labor, in the hospital they are encouraged to do what we in the West would call occupational therapy. Patients were seen folding bandages and preparing medications for the outpatient department, and doing work for a local factory such as making the covers of toothpaste tubes. The factory pays the hospital for the work done by the patients, and the hospital then uses this income to provide special services for the patients.

THE TEACHINGS OF CHAIRMAN MAO TSE-TUNG

Running through this entire gamut of treatment techniques is the philosophy of Chairman Mao. Inspired by his maxim, "Heal the wounded and rescue the dead," patients and workers alike study his writings, "On Practice," "On Contradiction," and "Where do correct ideas come from?," and the three constantly-read articles, "Serve the People," "In Memory of Norman Bethune," and "The Foolish Old Man Who Removed the Mountains." Patients are organized into study groups to study these writings daily. They are encouraged through these writings to understand "objective reality" rather than to function on the basis of "subjective thinking." They "arm their minds with Chairman Mao's thought during their stay in the hospital in order to fight their disease."

THE PATIENTS

In the psychiatric department of the Third Hospital in Peking—which has two wards, one male and one female, including 90 beds—we attended a performance given by the patients. The performance was given in a large room that they call their club, and was attended by perhaps 50 patients, who wore red pajamas and red-and-white-striped robes. Four patients gathered around a table to tell us and the other patients "How I used Chairman Mao's thought to conquer difficulties." First, a 32-year-old man with the diagnosis of paranoid schizophrenia spoke; he had been in the hospital for three months:

At the time of the last spring festival I had a quarrel with my wife. She said she wanted to divorce me and I was surprised. I returned to work but I was suspicious of my wife and kept thinking that she would divorce me. At that time my wife was not working in Peking and I asked to have her transferred to Peking and asked her to send my letters back. We quarrelled a lot because I insisted that she wanted to divorce me and she said that she did not.

During my early period of admission I did not know that I had mental trouble. Gradually I recognized that something was wrong in my mentality and I gradually recognized that I had to make a case analysis of the causes of my disease in order to facilitate treatment and prevention.

My trouble was that I had subjective thinking which was not objectively correct. My wife had not written letters wanting to divorce me; my wife actually loves me. My subjective thinking was divorced from the practical condition and my disease was caused by my method of thinking. I was concerned with the individual person; I was self-interested. I haven't put revolutionary interests in the first place but if I can put the public interest first and my own interest second I can solve the contradictions and my mind will be in the correct way. From now on I will study Chairman Mao and apply his writings.

The second patient who spoke was a 38-year-old grey-haired man with a friendly, open face.

My main trouble is suspicion. I think my ceiling is going to fall down; when big character posters are up I think it is criticism of myself; and when somebody is gossiping I think they are talking about me.

After I was admitted to this hospital I gradually recognized my illness. As Chairman Mao says, when we face a problem we have to face it thoroughly, not only from one side. When I am discharged from the hospital, the doctors have said that I should have some problem of investigation in my mind. When I am in touch with people they have suggested that I make conclusions in my mind after investigation not before investigation, in order to see if what I suspect to be true is just subjective thinking or is objectively correct. By studying Chairman Mao, we can treat and cure disease.

This patient was treated with chlorpromazine, 12 mg at noon and 14 mg in the evening. He also received consultation from a traditional doctor and was treated with traditional medicines.

The third patient who spoke was a woman in her twenties.

I was a graduate of junior middle school and in 1969 was sent out to work in an outlying province. I was admitted 5 months ago to this hospital but I am getting all right now. My main trouble is auditory hallucinations. I hear something in my ear saying, "What is below your pillow?" I found old magazines on the subject of a biological radio apparatus and I came to the ridiculous conclusion that a special agent is investigating me by means of this biological radio apparatus. I became agitated and heard loud speeches in my mind which gave me a very bad headache. During the midst of my torture I was sent to the hospital and received medication. My headache is much better but I still have hallucinations.

The doctors organized a study class of Chairman Mao's works and I joined the study class and studied the five works. I studied my hallucinations and gradually recognized that they were nonexistent. I found that investigation is like a pregnancy and solving problems is like delivering a baby. As I investigated my problem I gradually recognized that the biological radio was nonexistent. Now I still have some hallucinations but after ten minutes I recognize that they are not real. Now whenever I have hallucinations, I study the works of Chairman Mao and attract my mind and my heart so I will get rid of my trouble.

My treatments consist of acupuncture, medicine, herb medicine, and study. Also I am considering what happens in the whole world. I talk with doctors and patients; I do physical exercises; I have not completely recovered yet but I have faith I will get better and will win the struggle.

The fourth patient, a young woman who was a middle-school graduate with a diagnosis of schizophrenia, had been hospitalized for two months but had been discharged when her disease improved. She returns periodically for a checkup, and on the morning we visited the ward she had been invited back to talk with the new patients and to help teach them how to arm themselves with Chairman Mao's thought. She was dressed in street clothes and told us the following story:

I was a senior middle-school graduate in 1967 but my health was not good at that time. I had heart trouble and arthritis and was not sent out to work like my classmates. Last April I was called to have a discussion with regard to my work and I got my mental trouble at that time.

I was born in the new society and therefore have not suffered as people did in the old society. I was educated for more than 10 years and then rested at home for 2 years due to my illness. Thus I was divorced for 12 years from practice, class struggle, and revolutionary experience. I was a "hothouse flower."

I knew that sick people were kept in Peking and not sent out to remote areas and I thought day and night about where I would work. I had a fixed opinion that I had to work here in Peking, not elsewhere. I didn't want to eat and I didn't want to drink. I dreamt of being a People's Liberation Army woman at that time and had suspicions and fantastic ideas whenever I saw a member of the P.L.A. or a P.L.A. car I thought it would take me to the People's Liberation Army.

During my early period of admission I could not manage myself. I threw pillows through windows and had to be fed. I thought I was going to be poisoned here and thought I had to struggle against the hospital. When other patients sang Army songs I thought the P.L.A. was here already. Gradually I realized that the doctors and nurses were here to serve the patient. They washed my hair and clothing and I gradually realized that this is a hospital. I then participated in a study group and studied the Five Constantly-Read Articles for two weeks. I learned that my hallucinations and suspicions were not real and found that studying in a study class was a good way to solve one's problems. I understood that one has to have knowledge before experience and then try to understand objective reality.

When a member of the P.L.A. visited the hospital I thought it was for me and I raised the issue in my study group. The doctors told me it was just a visit by that member and it was not for me and I believed them.

I was discharged over three months ago and although my new job was supposed to be arranged July 1, it has not been arranged yet but I now have full faith in the Communist Party and the Government and know that they will arrange a job for me later on. Until then I will continue to take my medicine and have close contact with the medical people in this hospital.

The doctors at the Shanghai Mental Hospital feel that schizophrenia is the most common diagnosis of their patients. Over 50 percent of the patients are schizophrenics. The department also admits a small percentage of patients who have physical illnesses with psychiatric complications, such as those with disturbed liver function, epilepsy, and heart diseases. They feel that paranoia is the most common form of schizophrenia and that depression, catatonia, and postpartum depression are relatively rare. Suicide is also thought to be quite rare now. Both the Shanghai Mental Hospital and the psychiatric ward of the Third Hospital in Peking report that the most common age of the onset of mental illness is from 20 to 30. This corroborates the findings in the 1930s, when, in one study of mental illness, 40 percent of the patients' onset of illness occurred from 20 to 30 years of age (3f).

In a study conducted in the late 1950s involving a group of 2,000 schizophrenics, it was found that 50 percent of the patients were between the ages of 21 and 30; only 1.3 percent were under 15; and over 7 percent were more than 40 (4). Over 46 percent of the schizophrenics were paranoid, 24 percent were "unclassified," 15 percent were suffering from hebephrenia, and 11 percent were suffering from catatonia (4).

THE PERSONNEL

Before the Cultural Revolution, most psychiatrists attended medical school for five years and during the fifth year interned in a department of psychiatry in a teaching hospital specializing in psychiatry, internal medicine, and neurology. They would then remain in a psychiatric department of a hospital, learning the field further through doing "practical work," making rounds, attending lectures, and treating patients under the supervision of residents. A psychiatrist was considered trained when the senior doctors in his department felt he was adequately trained; there was no examination or fixed period of training. As medical schools have just reopened since the Cultural Revolution, a new pattern has yet to be established. The percentage of women in psychiatry at the present time is thought to be over 50.

Nurses are trained under the same basic principles. Again, before the Cultural Revolution they graduated from nursing school, during which they would have some psychiatric studies. They then had on-the-job training in the psychiatric ward to which they were assigned, which included practical work and some lectures.

The works of Freud are not and have not been used in the study of psychiatry since 1949. The works of Pavlov, however, have been studied, particularly during the period of Russian influence, but our hosts told us that without "considerable environmental and class struggle," the application of Pavlov's theories will not be effective.

HOSPITAL LIFE

At the Shanghai Mental Hospital, a Mao Tse-tung study class meets every afternoon for two weeks from two o'clock to three-thirty. Eleven patients dressed in brown uniforms sit around a table with one member of the People's Liberation Army and one member of a Mao Tse-tung Propaganda team who works in the hospital and takes part in the study class when he is free. One health worker is also present who is in charge of the patients' study group in this ward. They are studying the third Constantly-Read Article, "The Foolish Old Man Who Removed the Mountains." One patient tells the content of the parable, the story of an old man who had a mountain on his property and wanted it removed. He and his sons started to remove it with shovels, and his neighbors scoffed at him. But he insisted that if his sons and his sons' sons worked to remove the mountain, it could be done. He explains that they should all learn the spirit of the parable and put it into practice in order to strengthen their will and conquer their illness. Two of the patients sitting around the table are wearing red arm bands because they are on duty and their main task is to propagandize Mao's thought when new patients come into their ward. They tell new patients their experiences and help them get used to being on the ward. The patients who are on duty rotate so that everyone in the ward has a chance.

Patients live two, four, eight or sixteen to a room, depending on the severity of the condition. There were a few rooms with a single patient, and some of these were locked. The rooms are furnished very simply with beds, bureaus, and posters or slogans on the walls. The patients make their beds and sweep the floors with the help of the health workers. The daily schedule was posted on one wall and was as follows:

5:00– 5:30 A.M.	Get up and make beds
5:30– 6:00	Breakfast
6:00– 6:30	Occupational therapy
6:30– 7:00	Military training (Fridays)
7:30– 8:30	Study Chairman Mao's works
8:30–10:00	Heart-to-heart talks (Monday, Wednesday, Friday)
8:30–10:00	Study class (Tuesday, Thursday, Saturday)
10:00–10:30	Treatment
10:30–11:30	Lunch, free time
12:00– 1:30	Nap
1:30– 2:00	News
2:30– 3:30	Study class
3:30– 4:15	Physical activities (Monday, Wednesday, Friday)

3:30– 6:30   Visits from relatives (Tuesday, Thursday, Saturday)
4:30   Supper
Evening   Television
9:30   Bed

Exhortatory messages were on the walls as well. Lin Piao's quotation read: "Read Chairman Mao's Works. Listen to Chairman Mao. Work according to Chairman Mao's teachings. Act as Good Fighters for Chairman Mao." In another room of the Shanghai Mental Hospital a poster was on the wall, entitled "How to Prevent Disease Relapse." The first two items read:

1. Mental Disease is curable.
2. Being a psychiatric patient, you still have to study Chairman Mao's works hard.

The third point dealt with acupuncture, and the fourth point read: "Sometimes you will have symptoms. Don't worry. If you get treatment right away, relapse can be avoided."

In the patients' activity room they were playing Chinese chess and ping-pong, doing occupational therapy, and reading small comiclike books. A loudspeaker played a lively song from a modern revolutionary opera. Slogans hung across the room: "Hold High the Red Banner of Mao's Thought" and "Warmly Celebrate the Founding of the People's Republic of China." Those patients who are doing particularly well in their "struggle against their illness" have short essays written about them by the doctor and other patients, and these are posted on the wall. Also posted is the list of the patients who are paired together to help each other, the sicker with the healthier.

The average length of hospitalization in the Shanghai Mental Hospital is currently 70 days. The doctors feel that the relapse rate of schizophrenia before the Cultural Revolution was a problem—40 percent of the patients were likely to have two or three admissions. Currently they are emphasizing reeducation "right before the patients are discharged on how to deal with the environment and contradictions within the environment." They have also been conducting follow-up studies on relapse, and have found in one ward that was studied for one year that 18.3 percent of the patients suffered a relapse. Relapse was interpreted to mean the need for readmission or outpatient treatment. In a one-year-study of another ward, they studied 37 cases and found one case of relapse; this case was treated by treatment in the home and in the outpatient department. They felt that the most important factor against a high relapse rate is the Mao Study Class "to arm them with Mao's thoughts to better deal with the environment."

Acupuncture is considered a major method of treatment in the lowering of the relapse rate. The doctors at the Shanghai Mental Hospital have divided the criteria for success of acupuncture treatment into four levels: (1) cure—disappearance of symptoms, with the patient "managing everything by his own mentality"; (2) much improved—disappearance of symptoms with the patient "mostly managing by his own mentality"; (3) improved—with some remaining symptoms; and (4) unimproved. They recently studied 157 cases of schizophrenia for one year, and found that 74.3 percent of the patients were cured and much improved. They found further that 97.4 percent fell in the first three categories, that is, cured, much improved, and improved. Without acupuncture treatment they find a 70 percent relapse rate.

Because of the recent disclosures of the political use of psychiatry in the Soviet Union, the process of psychiatric hospitalization seemed an important one to understand. The doctors at the Psychiatric Ward of the Third Hospital in Peking say that hospitalization is nearly always through persuasion—the persuasion of relatives, friends, and colleagues at work. Admission to the hospital is generally a joint effort by the family and the authorities of the unit in which the patient works, and, usually, they all agree on the need for hospitalization. Commitment is occasionally by force, but this was thought to be exceptional.

After admission, the patient needs to be persuaded by the personnel to remain and receive treatment. The technique of old patients welcoming new patients and helping them to adjust was considered important in this beginning phase of hospitalization. As the patient recovers slightly, he sometimes must be persuaded to stay in order to achieve a thorough improvement. The doctors maintain that the patients never leave the hospital against the advice of the physician; they feel this is because the physicians obtain the cooperation of the members of the Revolutionary Committee where the patients work and of the patient's family. They stress that the patient respects the opinions of the authorities where he works, and if the doctor, the patient's family, and the members of the Revolutionary Committee all agree, the patient is likely to abide by their suggestions.

SUMMARY

Currently, the treatment of mental illness in the People's Republic of China is a process involving multiple techniques: traditional and Western medicine, group and individual relationships, professional and nonprofessional help, mutual help and self-reliance, and in-hospital and community involvement. Since the Cultural Revolution, new models of organizing patients in mental hospitals in order to "raise the patient's initiative to fight his disease" are being tried extensively. The writing and thinking of Mao Tse-tung underlies all of these efforts.

Several basic characteristics of Chinese society are critical to the handling of mental health:

1. The society is an extraordinarily cohesive one, and the effects of this cohesion have not begun to be explored with regard to the incidence and treatment of mental illness.
2. The organization of the society into small groups in which mutual help and local participation are emphasized must be seen both as an effort at preventive mental health and as an adjunct to the treatment of mental patients.
3. The belief in the malleability and perfectibility of man through "education and reeducation" is the foundation on which many of the new techniques, such as Mao Tse-tung study groups, are based.
4. Although the Chinese are attempting to fashion their own brand of mental-health services through using their social structure and their traditional medicine, they incorporate Western techniques, such as drug therapy, when they feel they are useful.

Throughout the Chinese medical-care system, as well as in other facets of life, the pragmatism of the Chinese and their willingness to experiment are highly evident. Thus, the treatment of mental illness in China is likely to be a changing picture, which we in the West would do well to observe.

REFERENCES

1. Veith, I.: "Psychiatric Thought in Chinese Medicine." *J. Hist. Med. & Allied Sc.* 10: 261–68, July 1955.

2. ———: "The Supernatural in Far Eastern Concepts of Mental Disease." *Bull. of the Hist. of Med.* 37: 139–55, March-April 1963.

3. Lamson, H. D.: *Social Pathology in China.* The Commercial Press, Ltd., Shanghai, 1935, (a) pp. 415–16; (b) p. 416; (c) p. 410; (d) pp. 109–12; (e) p. 366; (f) p. 411.

4. Cerny, J.: "Chinese Psychiatry." *International J. Psychiatry* 1: 229–38, April 1965.

5. Hatem, G.: "With Mao Tse-tung's Thought as the Compass For Action in the Control of Venereal Diseases in China." *China's Medicine* 1: 52–68, October 1966.

6. Lyman, R. S., Maeker, V., and Liang, P., editors: *Neuropsychiatry in China.* Henri Vetch, Peking, 1939, (a) p. 234; (b) p. 233.

10

THE IDIOM OF DEMONIC POSSESSION:
A CASE STUDY
Gananath Obeysekere

Chapter 10 concerns an exorcism ceremony in Ceylon. In this small, preliterate society, the ceremony of exorcism brings together the curative elements discussed in Chapter 7—the venting of repressed emotion in a collective setting.

"In every man of course a demon lies hidden—the demon of rage, the demon of lustful heat at the screams of the tortured victim, the demon of lawlessness let off the chain, the demon of diseases that follow on vice, gout, kidney disease and so on . . ." Dostoyevsky, *The Brothers Karamazov.*
The problem dealt with in this paper is a simple, though an important one. It can be stated briefly as follows. In many cultures, illness and its symptoms are expressed in a religious idiom shared by the community as a whole. What sort of personality and social consequences result from this initial definition of illness and its symptoms (especially mental illness) in religious terms? Recent writing on mental illness in non-Western societies has shown the importance of sociocultural factors in mental illness (1), and Jerome Frank has presented a point of view similar to the one I shall adopt in this paper (2).
I shall illustrate some of the interconnections between cultural idiom and mental illness with the use of a single case history. The case history is that of Alice Nona, a woman living in a village in the Western Province of Ceylon, possessed by a *mala yakā* (the inferior spirit of a dead ancestor). Alice Nona is a woman of forty who married a man fourteen years her senior at the age of twenty-seven. She has four children—the eldest ten years and the youngest three. The third child is a male, the rest are all girls. She first became possessed by *mala yakā* about nine years ago when she was three months pregnant with her second child. The first "attack" did not last very long. For a period of five years she was free from possession. Her illness recommenced when her fourth child was conceived,

Reprinted from *Social Science and Medicine* 4 (1970), 97-111.

ten days after her menstruation stopped. Since then, she has been continually possessed by demons and has enjoyed only intermittent periods of "normality." Symptoms of her *pissu* or "madness" are very much like other cases in my notes. At the commencement of her *pissu*, she felt "burning sensations" in her stomach "underneath the navel" and an ache in her jawtooth. She found it difficult to stand or sit and had to lie on a mat. These symptoms occurred two or three weeks before the crisis. Then her body became cold, she shivered continually, and she experienced auditory hallucinations of footsteps following her. In an interview she stated that she saw demons, black hairy beings with protruding teeth, beckoning her. Her husband said that in this state she hoots and shouts, "I can't stay here. I got to go. They are calling me." The ritual specialists generally agreed that she was possessed by her dead father-in-law, who is a *mala yakā*. The interpretation was easy, for the woman admitted this herself when she was possessed. The husband however denied it and insisted that her *pissu* is due to sorcery (*hūniyan*) done to her before her marriage. During her attacks, her father-in-law speaks through Alice Nona and demands certain things.

After her first attack of *pissu* the husband had a *pirit* ritual performed (where Buddhist monks chanted sacred texts). While the performance was going on she became possessed. In her possessed (*āvesa*) state she told the monks that her father-in-law wanted *pin* or merit. The husband subsequently complied and had several almsgiving ceremonies (*dāna*) for Buddhist monks and transferred the merit to his dead father, the *mala yakā*. These meritorious deeds apparently did not satisfy the *mala yakā* because for the last four years he has been continually possessing Alice Nona. Now he does not want *pin;* instead he demands pork (wild boar meat) and toddy. The *mala yakā's* demands for palm toddy were satisfied; Alice Nona's husband gave her a bottle of toddy, which she greedily gulped. She showed no signs of intoxication for it was not the woman but the spirit who consumed it. Pork was not given because the household has been vegetarian for several years. Even toddy was given reluctantly because the husband had given up drinking four years ago.

Alice Nona came to my attention when she went for treatment to a Buddhist monk who was one of my major informants. She was introduced to the monk by X, a kinsman of hers. The story was told to me as follows:

Alice Nona was having another bout of possession and consequent *pissu*. She was in an "unconscious" state when X visited her one evening. When X spoke to her for some time, she regained consciousness. She asked her daughter to make tea for X. X asked her what her trouble was; she then had spasms, shivered, and could not talk. X asked her whether her jaws were "locked"; she shook her head to indicate "no." X told the husband that she should be taken to the temple of monk Y. Then Alice said, "No, I can't go there"; she had obviously regained her ability to talk. X told Alice

Nona that he had come to invite her to his wedding. She said "yes" and again lost "consciousness." Then X said aloud, "If there is a demon, be prepared to go to the temple of monk Y because I have a *dāna* (almsgiving) in my house preparatory to my wedding"—implying that the patient had to be cured in order to attend the *dāna*. At the word *dāna*, Alice Nona (that is, the spirit in her) started spitting (a sign of revulsion, hate). X said, "Demon, be prepared to go to the temple to listen to the command (*ana*) of the monk."

Half an hour later, X hired a car and took the patient and her husband to my informant, monk Y. The patient, meanwhile, had regained consciousness; she was not told that she was being taken to the monk but to an ayurvedic physician (*vedarāla*). In the car, however, she again "fainted." While driving to the temple, the door of the car mysteriously opened. When approaching the temple precincts, Alice Nona started hooting like a demon: "hoo! hoo! hoo!" They went into the residence (*pansala*) of the monk—the patient had to be practically carried there. When the patient was placed on a mat, she simulated spitting by saying "thu! thu! thu!" The monk told the "demon" in Alice Nona, "You can't try your pranks here." The patient was seemingly not aware of what was going on; her eyes were closed. The monk brought charmed oil in a cup and asked the husband to rub some on Alice Nona's head. When her husband attempted to do this, she "unconsciously" threw up her hands and tried to prevent it. The people held her hands and the husband applied the oil. The woman was now quiet.

For one and a half hours the monk asked the husband for details about the illness, namely, Alice Nona's family background, information regarding her parents, the places where she had lived, details regarding her marriage, and detailed information about her illness. The monk then decided to obtain information from the patient herself. Because the patient was having her period and was hence polluted (*kili*), he could not take her to the temple (*devāle*) of the deity Hūniyan. They took her instead to a room in the monk's residence. The patient was placed on a mat, face up, with her head pointing north (north being the direction where the demons reside). The monk asked the woman to keep her hands folded on her chest (which she complied with) and her eyes closed (they were closed anyway). The monk now stood at the foot of the mat uttering continuously for two minutes, "Sleep, sleep, sleep, sleep. . . ." He then bent over the woman and placed his palms together, six inches above the patient's head. He drew his palms downward from the head of the patient to her feet three times. The woman was completely immobile, still, as if sleeping. The monk straightened himself and with characteristic virtuosity challenged anyone present to wake her up. X shouted, "Alice Nona, Alice Nona"; the husband curtly, "Ei, Ei, get up, get up"; but there was no response whatever from the patient. Others present tried to wake her but to no avail. The monk then said aloud: "I am calling you. You should not open your eyes or talk, only reply to the questions I ask you."

The following dialogue then ensued. Note in this account (as well as in the preceding events), the highly matter-of-fact manner in which the individuals involved treat the existence and presence of supernatural beings. They are simply viewed as part of the behavioral landscape.

MONK: "Now patient (*āturā*) you must see the Lord Vishnu. He will come to you and you must tell us what he looks like."

ALICE NONA (eyes closed): "I see him; he is blue." (Blue is the color of Vishnu.)

MONK (addressing Lord Vishnu): "O, Lord Vishnu, tell us what is wrong with the patient."

ALICE NONA (Vishnu speaking): "This man (that is, the husband) had not fulfilled a *bāra* (vow) to Vishnu for a blue altar cloth and a 'form' (*rūpe*) for 'form.' "

The monk now asked the husband whether it was true. The husband admitted that he had promised to give Vishnu a blue curtain and a form (*rūpe*, an image or form as a present for the God) if he would save the "form" of his wife. But since the God did not cure his wife, the husband did not feel obliged to fulfill his vow.

The monk asked Vishnu to depart. The patient said that Vishnu had left her. The monk now implored the Goddess Sri (the Earth goddess) and Valliamma (wife of Skanda) to speak through the patient.

MONK: "Here come the Goddess Sri and Valliamma."

ALICE NONA: "Chi! Chi!" ("Chi" is a revulsive exclamation in Sinhalese often associated with feces and dirt.)

The monk explained that the female deities would not come owing to the woman's menstrual impurity. The monk now asked the God Skanda to reside in the woman. He asked the patient whether Skanda had come.

ALICE NONA: "Yes, he has come (*vädiyā*)."

MONK: "Who is the being who is possessing (*vähilā*) this human life (*naraprāne*)?"

ALICE NONA (Skanda speaking): "Yakōris." (the husband's father's name).

MONK: "In what shape is he possessing her, oh God?"

ALICE NONA: "Mala yakā."

Now the monk addressed Alice Nona rather than Skanda.

MONK: "There are many gods in the Divine Company (*dēvasamāgama*); tell us for whom this *mala yakā* works."

ALICE NONA (herself speaking): "He is the servant of Skanda."

MONK: "Why is he possessing you?"

ALICE NONA (herself speaking on behalf of *mala yakā*): "For the love of the daughter-in-law and the hatred of this one" (*mēgolla*, "this one," i.e., the husband).

MONK: "Why does he hate the husband?"

ALICE NONA (spirit speaking): "He did not even attend my funeral."

The monk now asked the husband whether this was true. The husband said that he could not come to the funeral of his father because he was in jail at the time!

MONK: "Do you want *pin* (merit) or do you want food?"

ALICE NONA (spirit speaking): "I don't want *pin*."

MONK: "What do you want?"

ALICE NONA (spirit speaking): "I want toddy (*kitulrā*) and pork."

The monk asked the husband what his father's occupation had been. The husband explained that his father used to make toddy and hunt.

ALICE NONA (spirit speaking): "I pushed my wife from a rock and broke her back. Three days ago I broke the cow's leg."

The monk inquired about the background of these incidents, which I shall discuss later in my analysis. After this, the monk asked the husband to inquire from his father why he treats him so badly even though the husband had transferred much merit to his father and is now leading a good life.

ALICE NONA (spirit speaking): "You did not come when I was dying, you were no help to me. I will destroy you (*nätikaranava*). I will break your neck—I won't do it because my daughter-in-law is good. You scold her, you are harsh (*särayi*). I have told her to leave you but she won't because of the love (*ādaraya*) she has for you."

The monk asked X to speak to the patient.

X: "What is the relationship of the *mala yakā* to me?"

ALICE NONA: "No relationship."

X explained that this was true because X was related to Alice Nona only and she was not married at the time of Yakoris's death.

X: "Remember what I told the demon when we were at home."

ALICE NONA (spirit speaking): "You asked me to come to the temple. I said I could not. Then you cheated me and brought me here."

X: "By command (*ana*) of the monk I asked you to leave."

ALICE NONA (spirit speaking): "Yes, I remember. I opened the car door to throw you out and break your *botuva* (throat) but I didn't succeed."

The seance was now over. The monk sprayed some "charmed" water on Alice Nona and she got up smiling vaguely.

I have chosen Alice Nona's case to illustrate the clarity with which the dialectic of demon possession dramatizes the underlying psychological conflict in the patient. In her case, as elsewhere in Ceylon, demonic possession, as opposed to other forms of demonic illnesses, reflects serious "pathology" and is an attempt to solve intolerable psychological conflicts. This, of course, need not be the case in other cultures where conflicts resulting from the social structure and all sorts of minor stresses may be resolved through spirit possession (3, 4). In Ceylon, the same type of projective mechanisms—exorcistic rituals—may be used either for serious cases of possession or for lesser demonic illnesses. People are, however, aware of the qualitative differences involved, so that more elaborate and expensive rituals with "famous priests" may be held for serious illnesses. I am not concerned in this paper with the manner in which minor problems are culturally expressed or ventilated but rather with the way in which *serious* stresses and psychological conflicts are handled by the individual and his culture. The elucidation of the latter may also help us understand the former, but since this is a case study of the latter type there is methodological utility in viewing them separately.

How could an anthropologist *qua* anthropologist rather than psychiatrist handle a case like that of Alice Nona? One may look at her case from two related viewpoints: first, in terms of the modally present psychological problems faced by the group (in this case, resulting from the status of women); and, second, in relation to factors specific to the single case. Regarding the first, Sinhalese culture places a high premium on male greatness and superordination, and female inferiority. Submissiveness, chastity, modesty are the prime virtues for women. I have described elsewhere (5) some of the psychological consequences of the female role in another culture area in Ceylon. Though in the Western Province of Ceylon, from where Alice Nona comes, a greater formal respect is paid to the female, nevertheless the culture unequivocally defines the female role as inferior. Thus, the first set of factors relevant to understanding Alice Nona's case is the status and role of the female in the society, and the psychological conflicts they engender.

The psychological conflicts that arise from the status-role system are, however, not *role conflicts* in the sense of behavior ambiguity as a result of contradictory role prescriptions, or due to faulty internalization of role norms. On the contrary, the females may have learned their social roles quite effectively during socialization and may have learned to accept a great deal of the role prescriptions. When we speak of psychological conflicts generated by status and role, we refer to at least two things, among others. First, personality stresses may arise out of role learning in early childhood and continued role performance. For example, role learning may require drastic socialization of drives—in the case of the Sinhalese female, an excessive early and continuing control of sex and aggression drives through systematic repressions. The psychological consequences of role learning and performance may result in many women having hysterical dispositions. Second, psychological conflicts may arise through role evaluation, which is a function of the reflexive nature of the self (6, 7). The fact that role conflicts are not present, or that a woman has learned to play her roles adequately does not mean—as Evans-Pritchard (8) and, more recently, Peter Wilson (9) have asserted—that she would not have *psychological* conflicts regarding her status role, for this would imply an absence of a self. Self-awareness and evaluation are part of the very nature of the self and, by definition, generic human attributes. Role evaluation is facilitated when the culture itself provides alternative standards for comparison, as in the role ideal of adult males and children, older women, supernatural beings, and characters from folklore. Often, evaluative standards are built into the cultural definition of the role, as in Ceylon where the female is considered inferior (*pahat*, "low"), unclean (*jarā*), unfaithful (*avisvāsa*), and possessing polluting (*kili*) physical attributes such as the menstruation cycle. Finally, role evaluation can take place in reference to life, ideals outside of the role ideals of females, as in Ceylon where the life ideal of Buddhism is *nirvana,* but women are viewed as incapable of achieving this ideal unless they are reborn as men. Hence, one of the common prayers (*prārtanā*) of women is to be reborn as men in their next birth. Such views express criticism, evaluation of, and dissatisfaction with the female role, and an envy of the valued roles of men (and often children); and they are all functions of the self.

On the basis of the psychological problems arising from the status-role situation of Sinhalese women, we could draw certain inferences regarding demonic possession. The existence of hysterical predispositions in the personality makeup of women could lead to a general propensity toward expressing conflict in terms of possession and toward *accepting* possession as a culturally constituted projective system. The highly aggressive components in Alice Nona's "fantasy" are a reflection of the general difficulty the culture has in handling aggression. Yet not all persons express their problems in this manner, and, therefore, that they are common psychological problems of women is not a sufficient explanation. Moreover, the culture provides other "normal" means for coping with these problems, but these means were obviously not adequate for Alice Nona. Illness, whether mental or physical, is called *leda,* and as in the West, often qualified with an appropriate prefix to denote the type of illness. It is not a "normal" experience, as far as the culture is concerned, though it is an "expectable" experience. However, personality problems can be also expressed in ways that are not viewed by the culture as "abnormal." These would be in Ceylon, as elsewhere, through the individual mechanisms of defense; or through culturally provided defenses available to all, without such defenses being characterized as abnormal by intracultural standards. Pregnancy cravings of Sinhalese women, and the regressions involved during the early period of pregnancy, which I have described in an earlier article (10), illustrate this point. Another accepted way of expressing personality problems may be called *role resolution*. In Ceylon, for instance, a male homosexual with a transvestite predisposition may wear female clothes and become a stilt-walker. Or a frigid female may decide to join the order of nuns, and others may become priestesses of *deva* (god) cults or female seers. The adoption of a new status, and its attendant role, which utilizes and acts out the psychological problem of the individual in a positive manner, would be considered a normal way of "coping." Neither by intracultural standards nor by extracultural standards could we characterize these role resolutions as abnormal. But take Alice Nona's case, which is culturally defined as an "illness." Demonic possession for her is a frightening, traumatic experience and suggests the "abnormal" nature and intensity of her inner conflicts. When we interviewed Alice Nona, she looked physically emaciated and extremely depressed. She was able to talk at that time quite coherently and did not strike us as being psychotic in the Western psychiatric sense. She admitted to a tendency to retain stools; she dislikes passing stools and does so only once in two or three days. Her extreme depression had a strong component of self-reproach, as it is in Western society. Such sources of "involutional psychoses" would be expectable in a culture with a high premium on the repression of sex and aggression drives and the guilt-laden superegos of the women. Though "expectable," they cannot be common to the group as a whole, and, hence, we have to look upon Alice Nona's case as (a) an *intensification* of some of the present stresses arising from the status-role system or (b) as a result of unique life experiences or, as is more likely, a combination of both. What then are the factors specific to Alice Nona's case?

Alice Nona was the youngest of five siblings. Her father was a peasant cultivator living in a hamlet about fifteen miles away from that of her husband. She says that her father was both mother and father to her; she loved him dearly. She was not related to her husband before marriage. The husband had been in jail for fifteen years on a charge of homicide. He related to us the incident quite dispassionately; in a spurt of rage he had stabbed a man who had insulted him, and immediately surrendered himself to the village headman. His father, Yakoris, died while he was serving his sentence. After returning from jail, he reverted to a life of a hard-working industrious peasant. Since his marriage with Alice Nona, he had worked so hard that three years ago he had built a nice little cottage on a hill where they now reside. They had given up eating meat at that time. Four years ago he gave up drinking toddy. His wife's worst attacks started after they moved to the new house.

Our impression was that the husband was in general a considerate man, though he admitted that sometimes he had fits of rage and scolded his wife. He also said the wife is a good woman; she hates *sin*, dislikes people who drink. This was one reason why he gave up drinking. Alice Nona never complains of anything, he said. Even when she is sick, she says "nothing is the matter" and goes on doing her domestic chores. For her part, Alice Nona was distressed that her husband has had to spend about 3,000 rupees for her illness. She cried several times while I interviewed her and said she hoped she would die. That would relieve her husband and children of a terrible burden, she said, full of self-reproach. She spoke fondly of her father, who died six years ago. She sees him in her dreams; then she feels good. When he was alive, her father took her on pilgrimages. Now she hardly goes anywhere. Since her father's death, she has not even been visiting her siblings. They don't come to see her; "they are all well off," she said.

Several minor rituals were performed for her during the last three years; most of them were vows (*bāra*) to gods. On one occasion when they were at a *dēvāla* (temple of the gods), she (that is, her father-in-law) complained during possession that her husband did not care for his mother. The husband told us that this message from his dead father jolted him quite a bit, and so he went out of his way to please his mother. He sent milk from his cow to his mother every day.

One major ritual to banish the *mala yakā* was also held. During this ritual, the woman was made to enter a trance state by the priest. She was given a bunch of areca flowers; it was expected that she would whip herself with the long areca strands, but she did not. Then the priest caned her mercilessly instead. This ritual "cured" her for a period; it was during the very next attack that we saw the patient.

What was the nature of Alice Nona's psychological conflict? Her case was similar on one level to that of other Sinhalese women in the area: an inability to handle aggression and sexual drives, in Alice Nona the former more than the latter. The Buddhist culture in which she was reared also placed a high premium on nonaggression or *ahimsa,* especially in females. The woman is expected to be subservient to the parents and her husband, to obey them implicitly. Alice Nona seemed also to have a strong superego, witness her abhorrence of people who drink, and her strong religious bent. She also had several unusual features in her life.

(a) She married late, a man fourteen years her senior. The man moreover had been to jail on a charge of manslaughter. It was probably a difficult experience to live with a man with his background. Though her husband was now a reformed, hard-working peasant, he occasionally got into a temper and scolded her. This probably terrified her that she herself might be killed by him. From our interviews, we are sure that the husband never beat her. Many women in the area when beaten by their husbands retort with unbridled abuse (therapeutically beneficial!). Alice Nona was the uncomplaining type, keeping her feelings to herself.

(b) Her ontogenetic background was also somewhat unique. The youngest of five siblings, she lost her mother in early childhood. In such a situation, it is characteristic of the culture to emphasize her misfortune. Alice Nona would have been constantly told by others that she was an unfortunate girl, a sinner to have lost her mother early. This would have led to a lowering of self-esteem, evident in the self-pity that emerged even in the interviews.

(c) She loved her father who appears to her in dreams at "good moments." The early death of the mother put the father in a culturally contradictory nurturant role, making it difficult for a girl in this situation to relate to her husband later on. As long as her father was living, she had the security of contact with him and her siblings. Continuing contact with the family of orientation is a major source of security for women in this culture, and patrilocal societies in general, but with the death of the father six years ago this contact with her family of orientation ended. Her siblings, according to her, are well off and do not visit her. The loss of a loved father, then, is also a case-specific factor that enhanced her sense of "not being loved" and worthlessness, and the lowering of her self-esteem. It should be noted that the more serious continuing illnesses occurred one year after her father's death. The hostile and aggressive components of her fantasies—that is, her wish to have pork and toddy instead of merit—were also manifest at this time.

What functions are served by the definition and expression of illness and its symptoms in the demonological idiom of "spirit possession"? Spirit possession in Alice Nona's case is an attempt to solve intolerable psychological conflicts. It helps Alice Nona to cope with her problems, to give expression to her repressed feelings. Her inner conflicts are expressed through the agency of the demon possessing her. Projecting feelings into a demon serves various ends. In the first place, there can hardly be any guilt for the hostile feelings expressed. The patient is absolved from responsibility for these feelings; these are the works of a demon having an identity distinct and separate from the woman. Second, the psychological problems are expressed in a demonological idiom shared by the whole culture. The etiology of the disease is thus easily grasped; means for curing it are also available. There is a clear logical nexus between the causation of the disease and its cure. "Repression," "projection," "depression," "lowering of self-worth" are abstract terms that help explain certain psychological processes; the demonological idiom in contrast, reifies and anthropomorphizes these processes and relates them to the larger religious world view of the people. The inaccessible experiences of the patient are brought into the open and made existentially more real for both the patient and the larger culture. In the modern West, mental illness is often looked upon as idiosyncratic pathology; here, it is transformed into a publicly intelligible cultural idiom. The public idiom facilitates communication between patient, ritual specialist, the family, and the larger community. How can we explain Alice Nona's choice of the spirit of her father-in-law, whom she had not seen? First, the father-in-law's name was Yakoris, which is a derivative of *yakā* (demon). He had been a sinner—a toddy maker and hunter, an aggressive man through whom she could express her own aggression needs. More important, it was best possible to express her hatred for her husband in this way, hitting him where it hurt most. Thus, the spirit Yakoris blamed his son for filial neglect; failure to attend the father's funeral and minister to his dying needs are, according to the culture, gross acts of filial impiety. The son's protestations were of no avail; the spirit mercilessly drove the point home. The spirit scolded the husband for scolding the wife. The woman's repressed aggression drives received direct expression. Through the medium of the spirit, the woman expressed the wish to destroy her husband, to break his back, drawing attention to her own goodness at the same time ("the good daughter-in-law"). Characteristics of her own father were also probably projected onto the demon, who says he loves her. She probably recaptured through these means the lost affective relationship with her own father.

The patient, we gathered from interviews, did not get on well with her mother-in-law—another standard feature of the culture. Yet we noted that on an early occasion, the spirit accused Alice Nona's husband of neglecting his mother. Alice Nona's (the spirit's) view that the husband had no love for the mother was probably motivated by the wish to hurt him more—this time for neglecting the mother. Yet this produced an unexpected result, for it compelled her husband to send daily a bottle of milk—symbol of primary love—to his mother. That this "draining away" of affection from Alice Nona to the mother-in-law made Alice quite angry is evident from the "seance" at the monk's residence. Here, the spirit said that he had pushed his wife and broken her back and had also broken the leg of the cow that supplied the milk to her. The incidents referred to are as follows. A few years ago Alice Nona's mother-in-law fell from a height and injured her back. Three days previous to the "seance," the cow accidentally broke its leg. Alice Nona's hatred for the mother-in-law and husband was expressed by retrospectively interpreting these events as deliberate acts of hate by the "spirit." Her own wishes were vicariously satisfied in this manner.

In the context of demon possession the woman's repressions are, to use Dostoyevsky's apt phrase, "let off the chain." The therapeutic value of behaving like a demon—an aggressive being—for a nonaggressive, rigid woman must surely be great. As is evident from the preceding account, the possession context permits the woman to act in a manner that in normal life would be severely disapproved of, and to evoke strong guilt or shame feelings. In normal life she is a good Buddhist housewife; yet on the way to the seance she "unconsciously" attempted to open the car door. In the seance, under hypnosis, she explained this, probably correctly, as an attempt to throw out X and break his throat. She "hoots" like a demon, wants toddy and pork, highly un-Buddhistic and unfeminine cravings. She is acting like an aggressive man, her sinful father-in-law; yet, to reiterate, she is absolved from all "blame" because it is in fact her father-in-law who is acting thus. No doubt, the woman suffers greatly because the experience is also terrifying; but I am convinced that without some such projective mechanism the woman would not have been able to cope with her inner stresses. In this case, spirit possession is a last-ditch defense against personality disorganization and psychosis. (In that case her fantasy life would have been an idiosyncratic one, out of touch with the culturally defined reality situation.) The cultural fantasy is a substitute for the idiosyncratic pathological fantasy and loss of reality that often characterizes the psychoses. In the Sinhalese case, the belief in demon possession provides a ready-made cognitive structure that can serve as a replacement or substitute for the private, psychotic fantasy. Insofar as the "cultural fantasy" is a public one, the psychotic loss of contact with the outside world is minimized to a considerable extent. When the problems of the patient are acute, the cultural fantasy of demons may be inadequate and the patient may become psychotic in the Western psychiatric sense.

The existence of a culturally constituted public idiom for the expression of psychological illness is a fact of major importance. In the non-Western world and probably among Fundamentalist sects in the West, illness is often interpreted in religious terms, as in demonic possession or attack. Such theories of illness are derived from the total religious system of the group and are part of a publicly intelligible religious idiom. It should be apparent that when illness is defined in religious terms, it ceases to be something clinically isolable and separate from the totality of the patient's experiences and those of his group. The patient's experience of illness—whether mental or physical—is articulated through concepts such as sin, sorcery, and taboo violation, with the rest of his experience as a human being and that of his fellows. For example, take the hypothetical statement "I have sinned, therefore I am ill." My experience of illness, in this case, is due to "sin" (or bad *karma*, as a Buddhist would say). But illness as sin is only *one* of my experiences as a sinner; there are other contexts, having nothing to do with illness, in which I have sinned (such as stealing, taboo violation, and fornication). Thus, the concept "sin" articulates my experience of illness with my other sinful experiences, and also with other concepts derived from my, and my group's, religious system—expiation, religious merit, other-worldly rewards and punishments, and so forth. Thus, the "existential meaning" of illness is significantly different to persons in cultures that give religious interpretations to illness, in contrast with those that give a strictly "scientific" interpretation. (Among educated people in traditional cultures, religious interpretations may coexist with, let us say, a modern bacteriological interpretation.) In the case of mental illness, the religious idiom has a more specific and crucially important function, which I shall explain in terms of what occurs in Sinhalese society. My view is that when a person in Ceylon is confronted with severe psychological stress and is on the verge of a serious breakdown ("the onset of illness"), he will often attempt to express his problems in a publicly intelligible religious idiom. The expression of symptoms and psychic problems in, let us say, a demonological idiom is in itself an initial coping device or defense of the ego, an attempt to communicate to others what these problems are. Such an attempt wards off (temporarily at least) total ego disorganization.

The manner in which this occurs is of course important. I shall attempt to explain this by placing the discussion in more abstract terms. One of the problems that has vexed social scientists studying psychological illness in non-Western society is the question of normality and abnormality (11–15). The discussion of what *is* (intrinsically) normal or abnormal can be a fruitless one. One solution to the problem would be simply to specify operational criteria that prevent a person from relating himself to (a) his culture, that is, to the norms, beliefs, and values of his group; (b) to society, that is, to others as incumbents of statuses. These, one may say, are the sociological dimensions of serious abnormality, and the sociological consequence is *alienation* from one's culture or society. For these to occur—that is, when a person cannot relate himself to his culture or to his society—there have to be certain psychological prerequisites (criteria). These criteria that constitute the psychological dimensions of abnormality have been summed up by Spiro (16):

1. A cognitive disorganization: the patient cannot think clearly as others in his culture do; his cognitions are private, incommunicable, "a fantasy."

2. A perceptual disorientation: the patient's perception of reality is distorted; he does not see as others in his culture do ("failure in reality testing").

3. An affectual disorientation: the patient's affects are qualitatively different from others in his group.

If an individual manifests any *one* of the three psychological criteria, he will not be able *ipso facto* to relate himself to either his culture or his society or both. Placing this in the context of the preceding discussion, we would say that the initial expression of mental illness in terms of a public religious idiom wards off the first two psychological criteria and helps a person to relate himself to his *culture*, though not necessarily to the social structure. First, cognitive disorganization is warded off because although the patient may be obsessed with his own demonic fears, his thought processes are not "culture alien": others in the culture also believe in the existence, powers, and terrifying attributes of demons. If psychotic fantasy is self-communication in terms of a private idiom, here the patient cognizes in a manner that permits communication with others. No one in the culture denies the reality of these demons that inhabit their "behavioral environment," to use Hallowell's phrase. Second, perceptual disorientation is warded off. The patient, true enough, has visions of demons attacking him, but everyone believes in the existence of these demons, and, hence, he is not seeing objects that are culturally "unreal." To repeat, a "culturally constituted fantasy" acts as a replacement or substitute for the idiosyncratic fantasy of the psychoses. I am not, of course, suggesting that the patient's percepts and cognitions are identical with others in the culture; this is obviously not the case, for the intensity of the patient's experience and the strength of his projections are different from those of his group. Yet the experience is neither alien nor a difficult one for others to comprehend. Sociologically speaking, the individual is not alienated from his culture (see note 2).

Thus, although cognitive and perceptual disorientation is warded off through the public religious idiom, the third psychological criterion may be present; that is, the patient's affects are extremely intense, so that he cannot perform his normal social roles. Indeed, the adoption of the sick role entails the rejection of the social roles: the patient cannot relate himself to the social structure. In Alice Nona's case, during her bouts of illness there was an almost total suspension of her normal social roles as wife and mother—that is, an alienation from the social structure. Herein lies the further importance of the public idiom of communication. The patient can articulate and relate himself to the culture (belief system) so that others can act according to the cultural definition of the situation and grasp the nature of the illness. Family and community resources are mobilized in coping with the illness. Others can consult a ritual specialist who will diagnose the disease and prescribe a ritual cure. The goal of these healing rituals (which I cannot describe here) is to utilize the common communication pattern in order to bring the patient back to performing his normal roles, and to reintegrate him into the social structure.

In this paper I do not deal with healing rituals, but only with the manner in which illness is defined and symptoms expressed through demonic possession. The seance at the temple was not a healing ritual; it was simply a diagnostic session. One conspicuous symptom of demon possession is the fainting spells experienced by the patient. Alice Nona, like others from my field notes, was often "unconscious"; this was repeated in her seance with the monk. Yet in the latter situation she answered the questions asked by the monk. The seance situation was, in our opinion, one of hypnosis; it is a favorite device adopted by the monk to elicit demonological information from the patient. The monk calls the technique *mōhana;* the will of the curer, he says, subjugates the weaker will of the patient. In fact, he also used the English term "hypnosis" to describe this state. It struck us that the two states are strikingly similar: the "unconscious" state of the patient when possessed and the hypnotic state occurring in the seance. Though Alice Nona was unconscious, she was *unconsciously* (in the psychoanalytic sense) aware of some events in her environment:

(a) When X used the word *dāna* (almsgiving for Buddhist monks) Alice Nona, who was "unconscious," starting spitting.

(b) She "knew" that she was near the temple and shouted "hoo!"

(c) While going there, she either "unconsciously" opened the car door or "knew" that the car door had opened. The unconscious state of the patient was not a total blackout; certain events were being registered, certain actions performed. Moreover, in her "unconscious" state she acted automatically, in terms of the cultural definition of the situation. Demons are embodiments of evil, and stand opposed to Buddhist values such as those of compassion and nonviolence. Thus, Alice Nona (the demon), when confronted with the Buddhist temple and its associated values, behaved in the culturally expected manner—the demon expressed hate, fear, and rebellion, but he was finally brought under control and subjugated by the monk.

The view expressed here that a mechanism analogous to hypnotic sleep occurs helps us understand some other aspects of possession. For example, when a patient is in the "unconscious" state a ritual specialist performs charms and magical lustrations and tells the patient to wake up. The patient acts promptly; the message of the specialist is being communicated to the patient in some way or other. Again, in healing rituals the specialist may himself invite a deity to reside in him, and get into a "trance" state. He may dance and fall exhausted as if "unconscious." But the moment some charmed water is sprayed on him, he gets up as if nothing had happened. This cure is almost invariably effective. We noted earlier that when Alice Nona was under hypnosis, the monk told her that she should get up and then sprayed some water: Alice Nona woke up smiling vaguely. This again illustrates the similarity between the hypnotic state and the unconscious state of the patient. We are therefore justified in assuming that the unconscious trancelike state of the patient permits the release of primary process material; furthermore, the patient's mind unconsciously registers certain selected events in her environment. Thus, we think that the state of "possession," "fits," or "trance" into which the patient enters, when she has her bouts of illness permits regression, abreactions, and the release of primary process material. I am not sure whether I would consider this process as "regression at the service of the ego," as Gill and Brenman (17) do for hypnosis. But I am convinced that the definition and expression of these processes in religious terms helps the ego to maintain a hold over the regressive and abreactive processes that occur. Fundamentally, what is shown here is the ego's reliance on its environment. In possession and in ritual trance, researchers have noticed time and again the confidence and security given by the environment to the person possessed—such as the ability of the priest or the shaman to induce possession in others and turn it off when required. The patient knows that whatever he does, there will be others in the environment who will take care of him and see that things do not get out of hand. Here again, the communication idiom is important because the environment—priest, family, and community—can be supportive to the patient and tolerant of his "bizarre" behavior only insofar as they can grasp the nature of that behavior through a mutually comprehensible religious idiom. Thus, we can describe the process that occurs here as "regression under the control of the environment." "Regression under the control of the environment" can occur only if the ego has sufficient strength to relate itself to its environment, and this in turn, as suggested earlier, is achieved through the expression of symptoms, illness, or stress through a publicly constituted idiom of communication.

NOTES

1. This research has been aided by a grant (No. G.67–363) from the Foundations Fund on Research in Psychiatry, given to me when I was Associate Professor of Anthropology at the University of Washington. While thanking the Foundation, I must also thank Marvin K. Opler and Melford E. Spiro, who read an early draft of this paper and offered useful suggestions; and Edith Buxbaum, who referred me to Freud's 1923 article on "A Neurosis of Demoniacal Possession in the Seventeenth Century."

2. At the risk of some oversimplification, consider a Western patient who claims to be possessed by a demon. He would immediately be classified as psychotic, for the idiom in which he expresses his inner problem is not a culturally acceptable one. Yet in the European Middle Ages and even in later times (as well as in contemporary esoteric subcultures of the West), such an idiom of expression would have been perfectly acceptable (18). In the Sinhalese case, no one would consider the patient's case one of hallucination. In this sense, the modern Western patient would be alienated from his culture whereas his Sinhalese counterpart would not. Yet insofar as role performance is impaired, both would be alienated, temporarily or permanently, from the social structure. In the course of our research, we have come across patients in Ceylon whose inner stresses were so great that they could not utilize the common idiom, but could only express themselves in a totally new or a variant idiom. These people are completely alienated, culturally and social-structurally; they are often rejected by their kin group and may be put into an "asylum"—an act that expresses total group rejection.

REFERENCES

1. Kiev, A. ed. *Faith, Magic and Healing*, Glencoe, Ill., Free Press, 1964.

2. Frank, J. D. *Persuasion and Healing*, Baltimore, Johns Hopkins, 1961.

3. Messing, S. D. Group therapy and social status in the Zar cult of Ethiopia, *Am. Anthrop.*, **60**, 1120–47, 1958.

4. Lewis, I. M. Spirit possession and deprivation cults, *Man, J. R. Anthrop. Inst.* (n.s.), 1, No. 3, 1966.

5. Obeyesekere, G. Pregnancy cravings in relation to social structure and personality in a Sinhalese village, *Am. Anthrop.*, **65**, 323–42, 1963.

6. Mead, G. H. *Mind, Self and Society*, edited by C. W. Morris, Chicago, University of Chicago Press, 1934.

7. Hallowell, A. I. Self, society and culture in phylogenetic perspective, in *The Evolution of Man*, edited by S. Tax, Chicago, University of Chicago Press, 1960, pp. 309–72.

8. Evans-Pritchard, E. E. *Position of Women in Primitive Societies and in Our Own*, The Fawcett Lecture, Bedford College, London, 1955.

9. Wilson, P. J. Status ambiguity and spirit possession, *Man, J. R. Anthrop. Inst.* (n.s.), **2**, 366–78, 1967.

10. See (5).

11. Benedict, R. Anthropology and the abnormal, *J. Gen. Psychol.*, **10**, 59–82, 1934.

12. Foley, J. P., Jr. The criterion of abnormality, *J. abn. soc. Psychol.*, **30**, 279–90, 1935.

13. Wegrocki, H. J. A critique of cultural and statistical concepts of abnormality, *J. abn. soc. Psychol.*, **34**, 166–78, 1939.

14. Landis, R. The abnormal among Ojibwa Indians, *J. abn. soc. Psychol.*, **33**, 24–33, 1938.

15. Devereux, G. Normal and abnormal: The key problem of psychiatric anthropology, in *Some Uses of Anthropology, Theoretical and Applied*, Anthrop. Soc. Washington, Washington, D.C., 1956.

16. Spiro, M. E. Religion as a culturally constituted defense, in *Meaning and Context in Cultural Anthropology*, edited by M. E. Spiro, Glencoe, Ill., Free Press, 1965.

17. Gill, M. M. and M. Brenman. *Hypnosis and Related States*, New York, International Universities Press, 1959.

18. Freud, S. A case of demoniacal possession in the seventeenth century (1923), *Collected Papers, Vol. 4*, London, The Hogarth Press, 1956 (9th imp.), pp. 436–72.

Index

INDEX

No matter how you teach your courses—SPECTRUM BOOKS belong on the reading list!

Whether you prefer to give your students a broad survey of several key topics in sociology, or to approach the issues in depth for more advanced courses, you will find these **SPECTRUM BOOKS** suited to *your* teaching needs.

SPECTRUM BOOKS *offer convenience*—

Many **SPECTRUM BOOKS** present articles and essays that are unavailable even in the latest academic journals. With these **SPECTRUM BOOKS,** such authorities as Ashley Montagu, Zick Rubin, Peter Marin and others have virtually assembled the reading list for you, collecting the seminal writings on the most current and important sociological problems.

SPECTRUM BOOKS *offer quality*—

Whether edited or written by a single author, each **SPECTRUM BOOK** zeros in on a key issue—from deviance, sex roles, and ethnic identity to topics in social psychology—offering students a clear definition of the problem, a thoughtful investigation of its causes, and practical suggestions for its solution.

And—**SPECTRUM BOOKS** themselves are practical. They are quality paperbacks, reasonably priced for class adoption or supplementary reading, and available in hardcover for library use.

No matter what your teaching needs or the needs of your students, you will find **SPECTRUM BOOKS** described in this brochure to fill many of those needs with quality and convenience.

*Abortion...drug addiction...homosexuality—
are they really crimes?*

Victimless Crimes:

Two Sides of a Controversy

by Edwin M. Schur & Hugo Adam Bedau

Laws banning exchanges of such widely desired goods or services as drugs, abortion or gambling often create more problems than they solve.

In this volume, Edwin Schur explains why attempts to legislate morality fail to stop 'socially unacceptable' behavior. Hugo Adam Bedau challenges the basic concept of victimless crimes and the moral inconsistency in social attitudes toward these controversial problems.

Approaching the topic of victimless crimes from different vantage points, the authors discuss:
- the human, social, and constitutional costs of criminalizing such behavior.
- the complexity of making moral and legal judgments in these situations.
- the sociological principles that should underlie criminal legislation.

CONTENTS: Preface. A Sociologist's View: the Case for Abolition, *Schur*. A Philosopher's View: Are There Really "Crimes Without Victims?", *Bedau*. Sociologist's Comments. Philosopher's Rejoinder.
*October Cloth $6.95 (94169-0)
Paper $2.45 (94168-2)*

New books from Ashley Montagu—

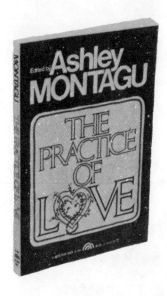

The Practice of Love

Edited by Ashley Montagu

In **The Practice of Love,** world-renowned anthropologist Ashley Montagu presents articles by anthropologists, social scientists, psychotherapists, psychiatrists, pediatricians, and others on the nature, power and importance of love.

This book reveals that love is the most vital of life's experiences, particularly during infancy and childhood. Montagu shows how unloved children grow up unable to love others and incapable of receiving love themselves.

The Practice of Love offers a humanistic interpretation of love. Montagu stresses the importance of love for individual growth, and encourages the reader to "practice the principles he acquires from the . . . many authorities who . . . have given us these new insights into the meaning of love."

CONTRIBUTORS: George Chapman, Ashley Montagu, Harry Harlow, Ian Suttie, M. Bevan-Brown, Brock Chisholm, Robert Southworth, Weston La Barre, Percival Symonds, Abraham Maslow, Rollo May, William Goode, Hugo Beigel.

November Cloth $8.95 (69447-1)
Paper $2.95 (69446-3)

On the power of love and the influence of cultural environment on development

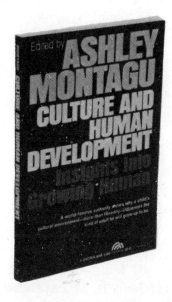

Culture and Human Development:
Insights Into Growing Human
Edited by Ashley Montagu

Ashley Montagu's new book provides graphic evidence that the cultural environment is one of the most profound influences on human development an individual can ever encounter.

In this volume, Montagu and other noted authorities examine examples of this phenomenon, showing that an unfavorable cultural environment—or a non-supportive emotional environment—can cause retardation, dwarfism, and other severe handicaps in children, while a favorable environment can actually reverse many of these effects.

The most thought-provoking insight this book offers is that "unfavorable environments" for children's growth are not restricted to "underprivileledged" homes. An emotionally deprived environment can occur as easily in a middle-class home as in a poor one.

CONTRIBUTORS: Theodosius Dobzhansky, Ashley Montagu (six articles), Rose Coleman, Sally Provence, Thomas Garth, John Rohrer, E. M. Widdowson, G. F. Powell, J. A. Brasel, R. M. Blizzard, John Reinhart, Allan Drash, Seymour Lustman.

October Cloth $7.95 (19557-8)
Paper $2.95 (19556-0)
A Human Development Book, Series Editors: Joseph and Laurie Braga

"Sex as we now think of it may soon be dead."*

*from an article by Marshall McLuhan and George Leonard in *The Future of Sexual Relations*

The Future of Sexual Relations

Edited by Robert Francoeur, Fairleigh Dickinson University and Anna Francoeur

The cloning of a complete human being from a single cell and even the creation of new species and sexes through genetic manipulation are some of the developments we can expect in the future, say the editors of this book.

Over the past two decades alone, effective contraception, artificial insemination, and transsexual operations have already radically altered our sexual relations.

This new book explores what the future of sex is likely to be, speculating on the effects of these changes on sex roles, parenthood, marriage, and concepts of morality.

In addition, contributors provide insights into the ways science and medicine, the changing status of women, and mass communications will influence our sexuality.

CONTRIBUTORS: Robert and Anna Francoeur, Rosemary Reuther, Marshall McLuhan, George Leonard, Alexander Comfort, Leo Davids, Raymond Lawrence, Jeanne Binstock, Roger McIntire, Sidney Callahan, Dotson Rader, Elaine Louie, Carolyn Heilbrun, George Ginsberg, Linda Barufaldi, Jean Rostand, Emily Culpepper, William Frosch, Theodore Shapiro.

October Cloth $7.95 (34591-8)
Paper $2.45 (34590-0)
In the Human Futures Series, Series Editors: Barry Schwartz and Robert Disch

These two books examine the changes we may soon see in sex roles and sex itself.

Men and Masculinity

Edited by Joseph Pleck, University of Michigan and Jack Sawyer, Wright Institute

Men and Masculinity describes how the masculine role is learned, how it limits men, and how men today are freeing themselves from it.

In this book, men speak from many viewpoints—student and mid-career, married and single, gay and straight —relating their personal experiences with the masculine role.

Men and Masculinity presents psychological and sociological studies that show how suppression of emotion and anxiety about achievement restrict men's ability to work, play and love freely.

Men and Masculinity tells of men's liberation. It shows how in consciousness raising groups and in their daily lives, men can help one another understand and transcend the traditional masculine role.

CONTRIBUTORS: Brian Allen, Ruth Hartley, Peter Candell, Marc Fasteau, Sidney Jourard, Julius Lester, Solomon Julty, Irving London, S.M. Miller, Robert Fein, Ben Cannon, Kelvin Siefert, Michael C., Joseph LaBonte, Jeff Keith, Don Clark, Robert Gould, F. Bartolome, Michael Silverstein, I.F. Stone, Gloria Steinem, John Gagnon, Barbara Katz, Stan Levine, Michael Weiss, Jack Sawyer.

October Cloth $6.95 (57431-9)
Paper $2.95 (57430-1)

In Patterns of Social Behavior Series, Series Editor: Zick Rubin

How to help children grow—
before they start school and after

Learning and Growing:

A Guide to Child Development

by Laurie and Joseph Braga, University of Miami Medical School

Children develop more skills and at a faster rate between birth and the time they enter school than at any other period in their lives. This book presents a practical guide to understanding and stimulating this development and growth.

The authors explain how to aid children in everything from learning to feed themselves to language and speech development. They stress the importance of helping children develop good feelings about themselves as people who can cope well with others and be successful at whatever they put their energies to.

Learning and Growing contains suggestions of activities and materials through which children can test and increase their competencies.

Application of these suggestions, plus encouragement, love, and respect, say the authors, will help any child to learn and to grow in mind and heart.

CONTENTS: Learning and Growing: An Explanation. Birth to 1 Year: Beginning. 1 to 2 Years: Feeling Their Oats. 2 to 3 Years: I Want It My Way. 3 to 4 Years: Age of Reason. 4 to 5 Years: Calm Before the Storm. What About School? Materials and Resources. References.
November Cloth $8.95 (52761-4)
Paper $2.95 (52760-6)
A Human Development Book, Series Editors: Joseph and Laurie Braga

"*The time has come to look at the pitfalls of deschooling, and this collection of essays prepares the way . . . The introduction alone warrants [its] publication.*"—**Ivan Illich** on **The Limits of Schooling**

The Limits of Schooling

Edited by Peter Marin, Vincent Stanley and Kathryn Marin

By its unswerving commitment to the basic right of individual freedom and personal growth, this collection transcends the more obvious . . . concerns of schooling . . . you are bound to profit from this sensitive collection and from both the scope and the depth of the issues being called to account. —**Mario Fantini**

Many people agree that our schools are in trouble. **The Limits of Schooling** provides a radical answer to what to do about it.

In this volume, Peter Marin goes beyond the idea of simply improving the schools. He asks whether we should replace our belief in schooling with a concern for the relation of children to the larger world . . . a world of experience far richer than that offered by pre-packaged learning.

CONTRIBUTORS: George Dennison, A. S. Neill, Jonathan Kozol, Paul Goodman, Ivan Illich, John Holt, Herbert Kohl, Sylvia Ashton-Warner, James Herndon.

November Cloth $7.95 (53693-8)
Paper $2.45 (53692-0)

Why people interact the way they do with others

Doing Unto Others:

Joining, Molding, Conforming, Helping, Loving

Edited by Zick Rubin, Harvard University

How do people influence each other without even knowing it?

Joining—What impels people to seek the company of others?

Molding—How is behavior shaped by the expectations of others?

Conforming—Why are people so strongly motivated to go along with the group?

Helping—When do people come to the aid of victims? Remain apathetic?

Loving—Why is passionate love often closely linked with fear?

Zick Rubin and other contributors provide answers to these and other questions in **Doing Unto Others.** The articles probe the dynamics of human social interaction and reveal the hidden forces at work in everyday social relationships.

CONTRIBUTORS: Stanley Schacter, Robert Weiss, Stanley Milgram, Rosabeth Moss Kanter, Robert Rosenthal, Lenore Jacobson, Nancy Henley, Philip Zimbardino, Craig Haney, W. Curtis Banks, David Jaffe, Solomon Asch, Irving Janis, Bibb Latane, John Darley, Carl Fellner, John Marshall, William Goode, Elaine Walster, Zick Rubin.

November Cloth $7.95 (21760-4)
Paper $2.95 (21759-6)

In Patterns of Social Behavior Series, Series Editor: Zick Rubin

*An exposé of American mental hospitals—
and a convincing argument for reform*

Circle of Madness:

On Being Insane and Institutionalized in America

by Robert Perrucci, Purdue University

Are those branded as insane really suffering from serious mental illness? Or are they casualties of a social order characterized by inequitable distribution of wealth and power— innocents who have become prisoners of the mental hospital system?

Perrucci takes the reader behind the scenes for a revealing look at the rigid social structures, traditions, and norms of the mental hospital, which are often used in place of sound treatment and release programs.

The author contends that hospitalization for all but those who pose a danger to themselves or others must be replaced by community-based treatment facilities, and that we all must adopt a more tolerant attitude to.vard those who are the victims of our 20th century American society.

PARTIAL CONTENTS: Preface. Communal Nature of Madness. Normality of Organized Madness: Everyday Life, Routines and Adaptations. Hospital Caste System. Bureaucratic Authority and Therapeutic Relationships. Patient's Release Ideology and Its Breakdown. A Search for Release Criteria. Victims and Caretakers.

*October Cloth $7.95 (13388-4)
Paper $2.95 (13387-6)*

A fresh look at white ethnic values and life styles

White Ethnics:

Life in Working Class America

Edited by Joseph A. Ryan, New York City Community College

Squeezed between liberal intellectuals and upwardly mobile blacks and Hispanic Americans, white ethnics have been made to shoulder an unfair amount of the blame for institutional racism.

Contributors to **White Ethnics** analize this and other problems faced by America's forgotten minority.

They reveal how white ethnics today are consistently overtaxed and underserved by government, their needs unrecognized and unmet by social and urban policy planners. This book calls for an end to society's unfair treatment of white ethnics, and stresses the social, political, and economic goals on which white, black, and Hispanic ethnic groups are beginning to work in common.

CONTRIBUTORS: Andrew Greeley, Perry Weed, Michael Novak, Richard Gambino, Paul Wrobel, Joseph Lopreato, Bill Moyers, Herbert Gans, Stephen Adubato, Richard Krickus, Leonard Covello, Peter Binzen, Gus Tyler, Raymond Wolfinger, Mark Levy, Michael Kramer, Nathan Glazer.

October Cloth $7.95 (95771-2)
Paper $2.95 (95770-4)
In Human Futures Series, Series Editors: Robert Disch and Barry Schwartz

How to use one of America's most precious natural resources — the land

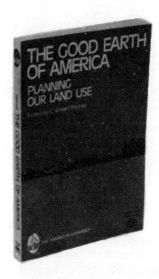

The Good Earth of America:

Planning Our Land Use

An American Assembly Book

Edited by C. Lowell Harriss, Columbia University

In this book, noted authorities take a hard look at America's land-use practices, revealing that our long-established policies of indiscriminate development make rational use of land nearly impossible.

Among other topics, the contributors discuss:

- how confusing laws and taxes have led to exploitation of the land.
- why the inner city is dying and what can be done to stop its deterioration.
- how the average citizen can involve him or herself in determining land use.
- what the alternatives are to today's morass of laws and regulations.

While the problems of responsible land use in America are complex, the contributors to **The Good Earth of America** show that they can and must be solved for our survival and the good of generations to come.

CONTRIBUTORS: C. Lowell Harriss, Carl Madden, A. M. Woodruff, Richard Slitor, William Shore, Donald Hagman, Lyle Fitch, Ruth Mack, Brian Berry.

Ready Cloth $7.95 (36034-7)
Paper $2.95 (36033-9)

Don't miss these recently published
SPECTRUM BOOKS
           on contemporary issues...

The Far Side of Madness

by John Weir Perry, C. G. Jung Institute

Challenges the outmoded approach to schizophrenia, in which the patient is drugged to suppress 'abnormal' ideas and emotions.

Proposes as an alternative an *intrapersonal* rapport between patient and therapist and a program of empathetic therapy to help the schizophrenic emerge a stronger person.

Cloth $6.95 (30303-2) Paper $2.75 (30302-4)

The Education Establishment

Edited by Elizabeth Useem, Boston State College, and Michael Useem, Boston University

Reveals the power structure behind our education system, and exposes the elitism that pervades America's schools and colleges.

Shows how power blocs and economic forces suppress students from poor backgrounds, while channeling economically privileged students into the 'best' colleges and the most prestigious jobs.

Cloth $6.95 (23656-2) Paper $2.65 (23655-4)

In the *American Establishments series*

Policing America

Edited by Anthony Platt, University of California, Berkeley, and Lynn Cooper

A myth-shattering analysis of the dilemma of the police today—caught between a hostile public and a political system based on repression. Shows how the police themselves are victims of the system, with contributions from the Knapp Commission, Jerome Skolnick, I. F. Stone and others.

Cloth $6.95 (68491-0) Paper $2.95 (68490-2)

The TV Establishment:
Programming for Power and Profit

Edited by Gaye Tuchman, Queens College, City University of New York

Views the TV industry as a business like any other, subject to the same organizational evils, governmental controls, and pressure to increase profits.

Reveals how TV propagandizes American consumerism, maintains the status quo and protects vested political and economic interests.

Cloth $6.95 (90240-3) Paper $2.95 (90239-5)

In the *American Establishments* series

The Poverty Establishment

Edited by Pamela Roby, University of California, Santa Cruz

Exposes the government officials and corporate officers who control the poverty establishment and benefit from it most.

Shows how this power structure creates poverty programs to regulate the poor, and preserves inequality by generating schemes to increase the profits of the rich.

Cloth $7.95 (69370-5) Paper $2.95 (69369-7)

In the *American Establishments* series

The Worker and the Job:

Coping with Change

**An American Assembly Book
Edited by Jerome Rosow**

Examines the attitudes and expectations of today's worker and describes the conflict between a society that is changing and a workplace that is not. Analyzes the causes of worker dissatisfaction and its economic results, and proposes solutions.

Cloth $6.95 (96536-9) Paper $2.45 (96535-0)

Ecstasy:

A Way of Knowing

by Andrew Greeley, University of Chicago

"Readers will appreciate the pragmatic analysis of mystical experience and its revival."—**Publishers Weekly**

"A practical work on an exalted subject by a hard-nosed sociologist. . . . stimulating. . . ." —**Best Sellers**

Cloth $6.95 (23494-8) Paper $2.45 (23493-0)

Tight Spaces:

Hard Architecture and How to Humanize It

by Robert Sommer, University of California, Davis

"A well-documented, statistically supported and readable appraisal of the effects of manmade public environments on people. . . . Encouraging and worthwhile reading . . . essential for the professional."—**Publishers Weekly**

Cloth $6.95 (92134-6) Paper $2.45 (92133-8)

Existential Sexuality:

Choosing to Love

by Peter Koestenbaum, San Jose State College

Is sex without love wrong? What about love without sex? How do family and children fit in?

Koestenbaum explains how practically any combination or rejection of these and other life options can be a viable choice, *if* the chooser faces the consequences of his choice fairly and honestly.

Cloth $7.95 (29493-4) Paper $2.95 (29492-6)

Spectrum Books in Humanistic Psychology, Series Editors: Rollo May and Charles Hampden-Turner.

How Do You Feel?

A Guide to Your Emotions

by John Wood

"This is a uniquely personal book. I believe anyone reading it will become more aware of the vast unknown world that lies within each of us. He will find himself more able to be, and to express those fragile things we call 'feelings.' It will encourage the reader to be more fully a person."
—Carl Rogers

Cloth $6.95 (39663-0) Paper $2.95 (39662-2)

Growing with Children

by Joseph and Laurie Braga, University of Miami Medical School

Shows how parents and all those who deal with children can best meet the needs which children experience during their development from birth to age six.

Describes each stage of growth the child experiences, given the proper support and stimulation, showing how parents can grow in understanding as their children grow in maturity.

Cloth $6.95 (36626-0) Paper $2.95 (36623-7)

A Human Development Book

Growing Older

by Margaret Hellie Huyck, Illinois Institute of Technology, Chicago

Demonstrates that social stereotypes of old age have little to do with the real alternatives available to us in aging. Explores the mental and physical changes, sexuality, relationships, work, and leisure patterns of older people, and offers a guide to how each individual can prepare now to lead a long, satisfying, life.

Cloth $6.95 (36777-1) Paper $2.45 (36776-3)

A Human Development Book

Managing Anxiety:

The Power of Knowing Who You Are

by Peter Koestenbaum, San Jose State College

Shows how an existential philosophy can serve as a basis of resolving many of life's problems—such as love, success, raising children, and coping with vague anxiety, guilt, and depression.

Explains how to build a personal philosophy, and how to gain insights which can be translated into action to achieve a freer life.

Cloth $7.95 (55035-0) Paper $2.45 (55034-3)

Spectrum Books in Humanistic Psychology, Series Editors: Rollo May and Charles Hampden-Turner

SPECTRUM BOOKS on sociology

BODY CONSCIOUSNESS: You Are What You Feel, S. Fisher, Cloth $5.95 (07852-7) Paper $2.45 (07851-9)

BODY LANGUAGE AND SOCIAL ORDER: Communication as Behavioral Control, A. Scheflen, Cloth *$7.95* (07959-0) Paper $2.95 (07958-2)

CRIME AS WORK, P. Letkemann, Cloth $5.95 (19291-4) Paper $2.45 (19292-2)

THE CRIME CONTROL ESTABLISHMENT, edited by I. Silver, Cloth $6.95 (19268-2) Paper $2.45 (19267-4)

THE CRIME ESTABLISHMENT: Organized Crime and American Society, edited by J. Conklin, Cloth $6.95 (19304-5) Paper $2.45 (19302-9)

CRIMES WITHOUT VICTIMS—DEVIANT BEHAVIOR AND PUBLIC POLICY: Abortion, Homosexuality, Drug Addiction, E. Schur, Paper *$2.95* (19293-0)

THE FELON, J. Irwin, Cloth **$5.95** (31423-7) Paper $2.45 (31422-9)

THE FUTURE OF WORK, edited by F. Best, Cloth $6.95 (34594-2) Paper $2.45 (34593-4)

GOING FURTHER: Life-and-Death Religion in America, J. Snook, Cloth $6.95 (35781-4) Paper $2.45 (35780-6)

LONELINESS, C. Moustakas, Paper $1.95 (54016-1)

LONELINESS AND LOVE, C. Moustakas, Cloth $5.95 (54025-2) Paper $2.45 (54024-5)

MYSTERY, MAGIC, AND MIRACLE: Religion in the Post-Aquarian Age, edited by E. Heenan, Cloth $5.95 (60903-2) Paper $2.45 (60902-4)

THE NEW COMMUNES: Coming Together in America, R. Roberts, Cloth *$7.95* (61247-3) Paper $1.95 (61246-5)

THE OTHER HALF: Roads to Women's Equality, edited by C. Epstein and W. Goode, Cloth *$7.95* (64298-3) Paper $2.45 (64297-5)

OUR CRIMINAL SOCIETY: The Social and Legal Sources of Crime in America, E. Schur, Cloth $6.95 (64389-0) Paper *$3.25* (64388-2)

PERSONAL SPACE: The Behavioral Basis of Design, R. Sommer, Cloth *$7.95* (65758-5) Paper *$2.95* (65757-7)

PRISONS, PROTEST, AND POLITICS, edited by B. Atkins and H. Glick, Cloth *$7.95* (71080-6) Paper $2.45 (71079-8)

PRIVILEGE IN AMERICA: An End to Inequality? A. Shostak, J. Van Til, and S. Bould Van Til, Cloth $6.95 (71111-9) Paper $2.45 (71110-1)

RADICAL NON-INTERVENTION: Rethinking the Delinquency Problem, by E. Schur, Cloth $5.95 (75042-2) Paper $2.45 (75041-4)

SEXUAL BARGAINING: Power Politics in the American Marriage, J. Scanzoni, Cloth $5.95 (80746-1) Paper $2.45 (80745-3)

STIGMA: Notes on the Management of Spoiled Identity, E. Goffman, Paper *$2.45* (84662-6)

TOWARD THE END OF GROWTH: Population in America, edited by C. Westoff, Cloth $5.95 (92579-2) Paper $2.45 (92578-4)

WHO RULES AMERICA? G. Domhoff, Cloth *$7.95* (95836-3) Paper *$2.95* (95835-5)